READING/WRITING COMPANION

Mc
Graw
Hill
Education

COVER: Nathan Love, Erwin Madrid

mheducation.com/prek-12

Send all inquiries to:
McGraw-Hill Education
Two Penn Plaza
New York, NY 10121

ISBN: 978-0-07-901837-3
MHID: 0-07-901837-8

Printed in the United States of America.

10 11 12 13 14 SWI 26 25 24 23   D

Welcome to Wonders!

Read exciting **Literature**, **Science**, and **Social Studies** texts!

 LEARN about the world around you!

 THINK, **SPEAK**, and **WRITE** about genres!

 COLLABORATE in discussion and inquiry!

 EXPRESS yourself!

my.mheducation.com
Use your student login to read core texts, practice grammar and spelling, explore research projects and more!

GENRE STUDY **1 REALISTIC FICTION**

GENRE STUDY **2 EXPOSITORY TEXT**

GENRE STUDY 3 ARGUMENTATIVE TEXT

WRAP UP THE UNIT

Digital Tools Find this eBook and other resources at **my.mheducation.com**

UNIT 4

GENRE STUDY 1 **BIOGRAPHY**

GENRE STUDY 2 **DRAMA**

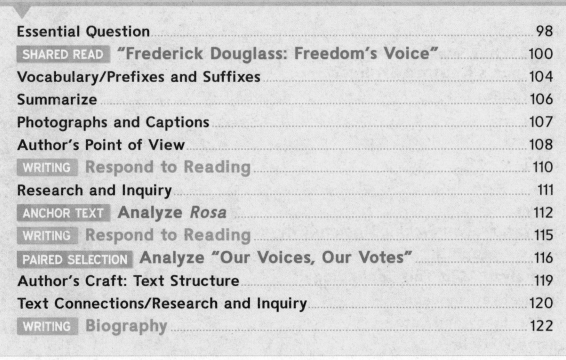

Todd Bigelow/Aurora Photos

GENRE STUDY 3 POETRY

WRAP UP THE UNIT

Digital Tools Find this eBook and other resources at **my.mheducation.com**

Talk About It

Essential Question

What can learning about different cultures teach us?

People in different countries around the world have different customs and traditions and eat different foods.

Look at the photo. The man is teaching his students African dance. The students are gaining an appreciation of the music and dances of other cultures. Talk with a partner about things you can learn from another culture. Write your ideas in the web.

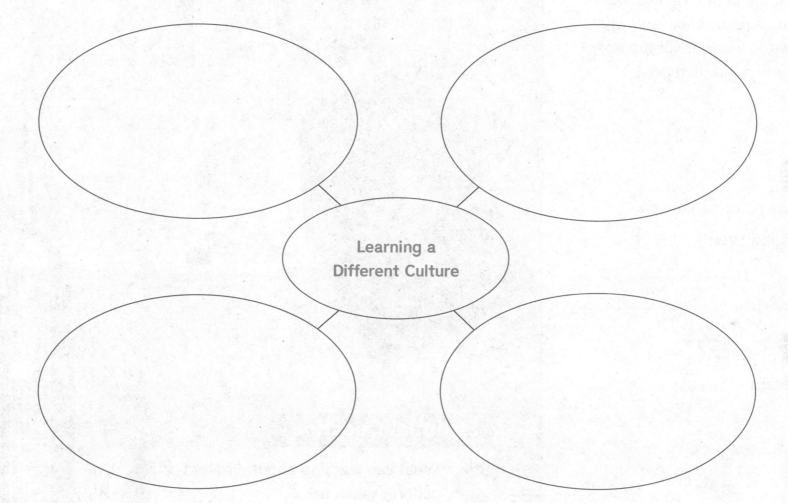

Learning a Different Culture

 Go online to **my.mheducation.com** and read the "A Special Day" Blast. Think about celebrations from other countries. What can we learn from these celebrations? Then blast back your response.

TAKE NOTES

You can set a purpose for reading by asking questions. Look at the title and the photo. Think about what you already know and what you want to know about the story. Then write a question here.

_____

_____

_____

As you read, make note of:

Interesting Words _____

_____

_____

_____

Key Details _____

_____

_____

_____

_____

_____

_____

A Reluctant TRAVELER

PASSPORT

United States of America

Essential Question

?

What can learning about different cultures teach us?

Read about what Paul discovers in Argentina and what he learns about himself.

(bkgd) Alan SCHEIN/Alamy; (l) Clement Mok/Photodisc/Getty Images; (r) Tom Chance/Westend61/Getty Images

"I think packing winter clothes in August is weird," Paul said, looking from his bedroom window onto West 90th Street. This wasn't going to be a fun vacation. He was sure of it.

His mom **contradicted,** "It's not weird, honey. Argentina's in the Southern Hemisphere, and we're in the Northern Hemisphere, so the seasons are opposite." To Paul, this was just another reason to want to stay in New York City. Paul wanted to spend the rest of his summer break hanging out with his friends, and not with Aunt Lila and Uncle Art in a faraway country.

Paul's parents, Mr. and Mrs. Gorski, were teachers, and this was a chance they couldn't pass up. Their apartment had been covered with travel guides full of **cultural** information ever since Mrs. Gorski's sister and her husband had relocated to Argentina six months ago. The Gorskis had big plans. Paul, on the other hand, wanted to sleep late and play soccer with his friends. They lived in a city already. Why were they going to Buenos Aires?

As their plane took off, Paul's dad said, "Look down there! That's the island of Manhattan. See? You can even see Central Park!" Paul never realized how surrounded by water New York was. Many hours later, as the plane was landing in Buenos Aires, Paul noticed similar outlines of a city on the water, and bright lights, just like home.

New York City

Buenos Aires

Cartesia/Photodisc/Getty Images

REALISTIC FICTION

FIND TEXT EVIDENCE 🔍

Read

Paragraphs 1-2

Dialogue

What can you infer about how Paul feels from what he says?

_____

_____

_____

Draw a box around the text that confirms how Paul feels.

Paragraphs 3-4

Theme

How does Paul feel and how do his parents feel about the trip?

_____

_____

_____

Reread

Author's Craft

How does the author's use of the map help you tell where Paul is going?

FIND TEXT EVIDENCE 🔍

Read

Paragraphs 1–3

Theme

Underline the text evidence that shows how Paul's mood improves.

Paragraph 4

Context Clues

Circle the context clues that tell you what *multilingual* means. Write its meaning here.

_____

Paragraph 5

Summarize

Summarize Paul's experience in the plaza.

_____

_____

Reread

Author's Craft

How do the photos help you understand Paul's experience?

"We have so much to show you!" Aunt Lila gushed when they met at the airport. They had a late dinner at a restaurant, just as they often did back home. But the smells coming from its kitchen were new. Uncle Art ordered in Spanish for everyone: *empanadas* (small meat pies), followed by *parrillada* (grilled meat), *chimichurri* (spicy sauce), and *ensalada mixta* (lettuce, tomatoes, and onions).

Paul made a face. "Don't be **critical,** Paul," his mom said. "Just take a taste." Though some of the foods were new, the spices and flavors were familiar to Paul.

"Mom, I had something like this at César's house," Paul said, after biting into an empanada. "This is really good." As he was **complimenting** the food, Paul felt his bleak mood improving.

Their first full day in Buenos Aires brought a rush of new sights, sounds, and languages. Paul noticed that like New York, Buenos Aires had people from all over the world. His Aunt Lila remarked, "We speak Spanish, but I really need to be multilingual!"

On a plaza, Paul saw a group of people dancing to music he'd never heard. Paul had seen breakdancing on the street, but never dancing like this. "That's the tango," Uncle Art said. "It's the dance Argentina is famous for! Being a soccer player, Paul, I know you have an **appreciation** for people who move well."

"You know, that is pretty cool," Paul admitted.

Around noon, they piled back into the car and drove to the most unusual neighborhood Paul had seen yet. All the buildings were painted or decorated in yellow and blue. "Soccer season has started here," his Aunt Lila said.

"Huh?" Paul asked, wondering if there had been a **misunderstanding.** "Isn't it too cold for soccer?" he asked.

"It's nearly spring. And," his aunt added, "Boca and River are playing at La Bombonera, the famous stadium, this afternoon." She held out her hand, which held five tickets to see these big teams play. Paul couldn't believe it.

"We're in the neighborhood of La Bombonera," Uncle Art said. "When Boca beats their rival, River, the people decorate their neighborhood in Boca colors!"

"Maybe I could paint my room in soccer team colors!" Paul **blurted.**

His mom smiled. "I **congratulate** you, Paul! You've turned out to be a really great traveler." Paul smiled, too.

Summarize

Use your notes to write a summary of the most important events in Paul's trip to Buenos Aires.

FIND TEXT EVIDENCE

Read

Paragraphs 1-4
Summarize
Summarize Paul's reaction to what he saw and heard on the drive.

_____

_____

_____

_____

_____

Paragraphs 5-7
Theme
How does Paul change by the end of the story? **Underline** text evidence.

_____

_____

_____

Reread

Author's Craft
Do you think "The Reluctant Traveler" is a good title for this story? Explain your answer.

Vocabulary

Use the example sentences to talk with a partner about each word. Then answer the questions.

appreciation

Gram showed her **appreciation** for my help by giving me a hug.

How do you show appreciation for someone's help?

_____

_____

blurted

By mistake, I **blurted** out the secret about the surprise.

How do you feel if you have blurted out a secret?

_____

_____

complimenting

Complimenting me when I do well makes me feel great.

If you were complimenting a friend, what would you say?

_____

_____

congratulate

After Niki lost the game, she went over to **congratulate** the winner.

What might you congratulate someone for?

_____

_____

contradicted

The children **contradicted** each other when they explained how the lamp broke.

Why might people have contradicted themselves?

_____

_____

Build Your Word List Pick a word you found interesting in the selection you read. Look up synonyms and antonyms of the word in a thesaurus and write them in your writer's notebook.

critical

A **critical** person often finds fault with what others do and points it out.

When have you been critical of yourself?

_____

_____

_____

cultural

Languages, foods, and celebrations are examples of **cultural** differences.

Give two examples of cultural activities.

_____

_____

_____

misunderstanding

Mira arrived at the show an hour late as a result of a **misunderstanding**.

How would you handle a misunderstanding with a friend?

_____

_____

Context Clues

When you don't know the meaning of an unfamiliar or multiple-meaning word, you can look for **cause-and-effect relationships** between words as clues to determine the word's meaning. Cause-and-effect clues may be within or beyond the same sentence as the unknown word.

🔍 FIND TEXT EVIDENCE

To understand what hemisphere *means, I can look at a cause-and-effect relationship.* Hemisphere *has to do with a location on Earth. Since seasons in the Northern and Southern hemispheres are opposite,* hemisphere *must refer to areas divided by the equator.*

"Argentina's in the Southern hemisphere, and we're in the Northern hemisphere, so the seasons are opposite."

Your Turn Use cause-and-effect relationships as clues to the meanings of the following words from "A Reluctant Traveler."

relocated, page 3 _____

bleak, page 4 _____

Summarize

When you summarize a story, you tell the important events and details in your own words. This helps you remember what you have read. It will also help to develop and deepen your understanding. You can summarize a story after you've finished it, or summarize parts of a story while you are reading it.

🔍 FIND TEXT EVIDENCE

You can monitor your understanding of the opening of "A Reluctant Traveler" on page 3 by summarizing the important events and details.

Page 3

"I think packing winter clothes in August is weird," Paul said, looking from his bedroom window onto West 90th Street. This wasn't going to be a fun vacation. He was sure of it.

His mom **contradicted**, "It's not weird, honey. Argentina's in the Southern hemisphere, and we're in the Northern hemisphere, so the seasons are opposite." To Paul, this was just another reason to want to stay in New York City.

As the story begins, Paul is packing to go on a family vacation in Argentina. He doesn't understand why he needs winter clothes in August. His mom explains why the seasons are different between New York and Argentina.

Your Turn Summarize Paul's first night in Buenos Aires and how the experiences affect him.

_____

_____

_____

_____

_____

_____

Dialogue

The selection "A Reluctant Traveler" is realistic fiction. Realistic fiction tells about characters that are like real people and includes their relationships and conflicts. The story happens in a setting that is real or seems real and has events that could happen in real life. Authors of realistic fiction may include interesting dialogue.

FIND TEXT EVIDENCE

I can tell that "A Reluctant Traveler" is realistic fiction. Paul and his parents travel from New York City to Buenos Aires, which are both real places. Visiting relatives and sightseeing are details that could happen in real life, and the dialogue shows what real people might say.

Readers to Writers

Dialogue often reveals the thoughts and feelings of a character. It can also help readers analyze conflicts among characters. For example, Paul makes a face after his uncle orders the local food. Paul's mother says, "Don't be critical," and tells him to take a taste. This conflict shows that Paul and his mother start out with different ideas about visiting new places. Think about how you can use dialogue in your own writing.

Page 3

"I think packing winter clothes in August is weird," Paul said, looking from his bedroom window onto West 90th Street. This wasn't going to be a fun vacation. He was sure of it.

His mom **contradicted**, "It's not weird, honey. Argentina's in the Southern Hemisphere, and we're in the Northern Hemisphere, so the seasons are opposite." To Paul, this was just another reason to want to stay in New York City. Paul wanted to spend the rest of his summer break hanging out with his friends, and not with Aunt Lila and Uncle Art in a faraway country.

Paul's parents, Mr. and Mrs. Gorski, were teachers, and this was a chance they couldn't pass up. Their apartment had been covered with travel guides full of **cultural** information ever since Mrs. Gorski's sister and her husband had relocated to Argentina six months ago. The Gorskis had big plans. Paul, on the other hand, wanted to sleep late and play soccer with his friends. They lived in a city already. Why were they going to Buenos Aires?

As their plane took off, Paul's dad said, "Look down there! That's the island of Manhattan. See? You can even see Central Park!" Paul never realized how surrounded by water New York was. Many hours later, as the plane was landing in Buenos Aires, Paul noticed similar outlines of a city on the water, and bright lights, just like home.

Dialogue

Dialogue is the exact words the characters say.

Dialogue is shown using quotation marks.

A new paragraph indicates a different speaker.

COLLABORATE

Your Turn Read aloud a line of dialogue in "A Reluctant Traveler." How is the dialogue realistic? What does the line reveal about the character?

_____

_____

_____

Theme

The **theme** of a story is an overall idea or message about life that the author wants the reader to know. Themes are not stated, but you can find them by thinking about what characters say and do and what happens to them. The settings and plots of stories can also help you to identify themes.

FIND TEXT EVIDENCE

When I read what Paul says in the first paragraph on page 3 of "A Reluctant Traveler," I see that Paul is not looking forward to his summer vacation. In the next paragraph, I see that his parents are taking him to Argentina to visit his aunt and uncle.

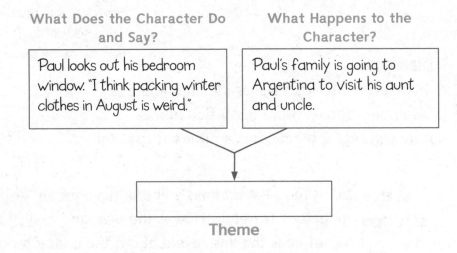

What Does the Character Do and Say?	What Happens to the Character?
Paul looks out his bedroom window. "I think packing winter clothes in August is weird."	Paul's family is going to Argentina to visit his aunt and uncle.

Theme

Your Turn Reread "A Reluctant Traveler." Complete the graphic organizer on page 11 by recording the most important things the characters do and say and what happens to them. Be sure to include specific ideas in the text. Then state a theme of the story in the last box.

New York City

Buenos Aires

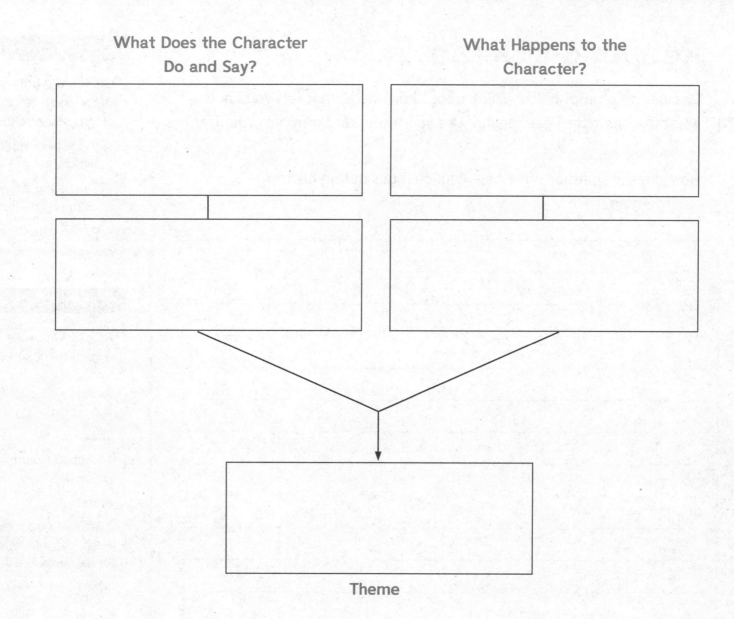

What Does the Character
Do and Say?

What Happens to the
Character?

Theme

Respond to Reading

Discuss the prompt below. Think about how the author lets you know what the characters are feeling. Use your notes and graphic organizer.

How does the author show how Paul changes during his trip to Argentina?

_____

_____

_____

_____

_____

_____

_____

_____

_____

_____

_____

_____

_____

Quick Tip

Use these sentence starters to retell the story and to organize ideas.

- *In the beginning of the story. . .*
- *The author shows Paul changing by. . .*
- *At the end, the author. . .*

Grammar Connections

As you write your response, make sure that the subjects of your sentences agree with your verbs.

Singular

*The **smell** from the kitchen **is** familiar.*

Plural

*The **smells** from the kitchen **are** familiar.*

SOCIAL STUDIES

Identify and Gather Information

When you research a topic, first narrow your focus. This helps you identify sources that have relevant information. When you **identify and gather relevant information** from a variety of sources:

- think about the purpose of your research
- make an outline or a list of main ideas
- take notes on the information you need
- list the best resources so you can go back to them, if necessary

What else would help you identify and gather information from a variety of sources?

> A. Celebrations
> 1. food
> 2. music and dance
> 3. stories

The partial outline above shows one student's categories to help focus her research about celebrations.

COLLABORATE

Create a Pamphlet With a partner, research celebrations, customs, and traditions of a group of people. Then create a pamphlet that presents and summarizes the information. Think about these clarifying questions when preparing your pamphlet:

- Which celebrations, customs, and traditions do you want to focus on?
- Is there someone well known for sharing these customs and traditions?

Discuss how you will gather information from websites, books, or people. Have an adult help you develop and follow a research plan. Plan what to include in your pamphlet, such as photos and captions. After you complete your pamphlet, you will present it to your class.

Quick Tip

There are two ways to gather information during research. Formal inquiry means using encyclopedias, books, and reliable websites. Informal inquiry means talking to people, such as neighbors or relatives, to get information. You should ask and clarify questions through informal inquiry. The adults you talk to during informal inquiry can help you develop and follow a research plan.

They Don't Mean It!

? How does the author show that Mary's mother does not feel like she is being true to her culture?

Literature Anthology: pages 182–193

Talk About It Reread paragraph 5 on **Literature Anthology** page 184. Turn to a partner and talk about how Mary describes her mother.

Cite Text Evidence What clues show that Mary's mother is not keeping her Chinese traditions? Write text evidence in the chart.

Evaluate Information

The author uses the expression "made her soft" to describe Mary's mother. Think about what it means to become "soft." Why would readers think that Mrs. Yang is not becoming soft?

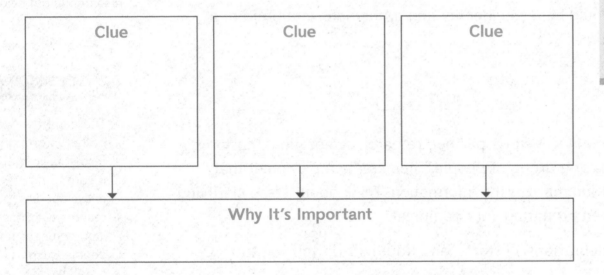

Clue	Clue	Clue

Why It's Important

Write I know that Mary's mother feels like she is not being true to her culture because the author _____

_____

_____

? **How does the author use dialogue to help you understand a conflict between Mary and her mother?**

COLLABORATE

Talk About It Reread paragraphs 4-6 on **Literature Anthology** page 187. Turn to a partner and talk about what Mary and her mother discuss.

Cite Text Evidence What do Mary and her mother say and how does it show the conflict? Write text evidence in the chart.

Text Evidence	What It Shows

Write The dialogue shows the conflict between Mary and her mother by

_____

_____

_____

_____

Make Inferences

Paying attention to the characters' relationships with one another will help you infer information about them. In paragraph 4, think about why Mary doesn't tell Mrs. O'Meara how much work it was to make the salad. What does this tell you about the kind of person Mary is?

? **How does the author use the illustration to show how Mrs. Yang has changed?**

Talk About It Reread paragraph 4 on **Literature Anthology** page 193. Use clues from the text and illustration to discuss what Mrs. Yang does.

Cite Text Evidence What clues in the text and illustration help you see how Mrs. Yang has changed? Write evidence in the chart.

Text Evidence	Illustration Clues	What It Shows

Write The author uses the illustration to show that Mrs. Yang has changed by _____

_____

_____

_____

Quick Tip

When you read a text, analyze the author's use of graphic features, such as illustrations. Paying close attention to how the characters are shown will help you understand how they feel.

Respond to Reading

Discuss the prompt below. Apply your own knowledge of what it is like to learn about a new culture to inform your answer. Use your notes and graphic organizer.

How does the author show how the Yangs change as they try to find a balance between their Chinese traditions and their new American life?

_____

_____

_____

_____

_____

_____

_____

_____

_____

_____

Quick Tip

Use these sentence starters to help organize your text evidence.

- *The author uses dialogue to show. . .*
- *The illustrations help me to see. . .*
- *This helps me understand how the Yangs. . .*

Self-Selected Reading

Choose a text and fill in your writer's notebook with the title, author, and genre. Record your purpose for reading. For example, you may be reading to answer a question or for entertainment.

Where Did That Come From?

Literature Anthology:
pages 196–197

From Bite...

1   Food is one of the most common ways people have shared cultures. Dishes we think of as American have in fact come from all over the world. Hamburgers were crafted by German immigrants. Macaroni was rolled out by Italians. Apple pie was first served not in America but England.

...To Beat

2   People from different backgrounds have also drummed distinct sounds into the music we hear today. Hip hop and rap, for example, have been traced to West African and Caribbean storytelling. Salsa music comes from a type of Cuban music called "son," which has been linked to both Spanish and African cultures. These unique genres owe their rhythms to the drum. This instrument can be found in nearly every culture in the world.

Reread the first heading. **Underline** clues in paragraph 1 that show this is a good heading for the section.

COLLABORATE

Reread the second heading. Analyze how the author shows that both paragraphs are related. **Circle** what the author does to help you see that.

In paragraph 2, **draw a box** around the sentence that helps you understand the heading. How does the author support his choice for the heading? **Circle** the text evidence. Write it here:

1. _____

2. _____

3. _____

United in Sports

3　Even the sports we play have come from other places. Soccer's origins have been connected with a number of countries, including Italy and China. Tennis likely came from France, but some think it may have even been played in ancient Egypt. While no one may know the exact origin of some of these sports, there is no doubt they are now considered popular American activities.

4　Our nation has been enriched by a diversity of cultures. Learning the origins of what makes up American culture can lead to a new appreciation for the people and places from which they come.

Reread the excerpt. **Circle** two examples the author uses to support the heading of this section.

COLLABORATE

Talk with a partner about why "United in Sports" is a good heading. **Make a mark** in the margin beside the text evidence that supports your discussion.

Reread paragraph 4. **Underline** two benefits of diversity in our country. Write them here:

1. _____

2. _____

_____

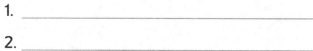

iStockphoto/Getty Images

How do the headings help you understand the influence of other cultures on America?

Talk About It Reread the headings on pages 18–19. With a partner, talk about how they are related and what the author wants you to understand.

Cite Text Evidence What text evidence shows that the headings and text are related? Write it in the chart.

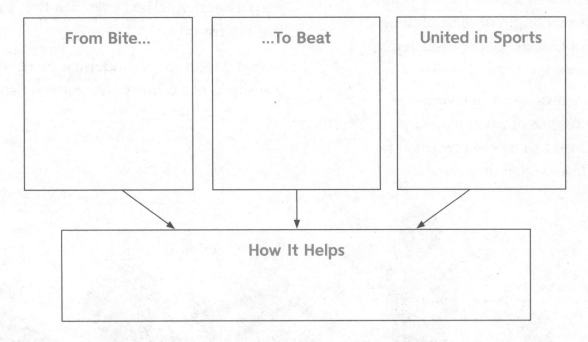

From Bite...	...To Beat	United in Sports

How It Helps

Write The headings help me understand _____

_____

_____

_____

Author's Purpose

An author has a purpose, or reason, for writing. When you read a text, think about what the author wants readers to know and why the author wants them to know this.

FIND TEXT EVIDENCE

Good writers do not use stereotypes. A stereotype is an oversimplified belief about a certain person, group, or issue. The purpose of stereotyping is to present a conventional image or opinion. The author of "Where Did That Come From?" tells about groups of people but stays away from stereotypes. Instead, the author tells how different groups have contributed to American culture. On page 18, the author uses the words "in fact" to correct stereotypes about some American dishes.

> Dishes we think of as American have in fact come from all over the world. Hamburgers were crafted by German immigrants. Macaroni was rolled out by Italians.

Your Turn Reread paragraph 3 on page 19.

- What is the author's purpose? _____

  _____

- How do you know this is the author's purpose? _____

  _____

  _____

The main purposes for writing are to entertain, to inform, or to persuade. Sometimes authors do not directly state everything. You may need to infer the author's purpose by evaluating the details in the text.

Text Connections

? How do Frances Frost and the authors of *They Don't Mean It!* and "Where Did That Come From?" help you understand their messages about other cultures?

Quick Tip

The song below is written in both Portuguese and English. How would the meaning of the song change if it were in only one language?

Talk About It With a partner, read the song lyrics. Talk about why Frances Frost presents the song in two languages.

COLLABORATE

Cite Text Evidence **Circle** clues in the song that tell what the singer is doing. **Underline** details that show the result of the singer's actions. **Draw a box around** the songwriter's reason for taking action. Think about what the songwriter wants you to know.

Write The songwriter and authors share their messages by _____

_____

_____

_____

_____

_____

_____

De Lanterna na Mão
(With a Lantern in My Hand)

Eu procurei,
de lanterna na mão,
procurei, procurei, e achei
Você para o meu coração.
(repeat)

E agora, e agora
eu vou jogar
minha lanterna fora. (repeat)

I search for you with a lantern in my hand.
Searching here, searching there
and at last I find you, and you are my friend.
(repeat)

I have found you, I have found you
and now I can throw away my lantern.
(repeat)

— Frances Frost

SOCIAL STUDIES

Present Your Work

COLLABORATE

Discuss how you will present your pamphlet about the customs and traditions of a group of people. Use the Presenting Checklist as you practice your presentation. Discuss the sentence starters below and write your answers.

An interesting fact I learned was _____

_____

_____

I would like to research more about _____

_____

_____

FatCamera/E+/Getty Images

Expert Model

Literature Anthology: pages 182–193

Features of Realistic Fiction

Realistic fiction tells about things that could happen in real life. Realistic fiction

- has characters that could be real people and includes realistic dialogue

- has settings that are real or seem real

- has a sequence of events, or plot, that could happen in real life

Analyze an Expert Model Studying realistic fiction will help you learn how to write realistic fiction of your own. **Reread** the first four paragraphs of *They Don't Mean It!* on page 183 in the **Literature Anthology**. Write your answers to the questions below.

What details tell you that *They Don't Mean It!* is realistic fiction?

_____

_____

_____

What kind of person is Father? What details from the text tell you that?

_____

_____

_____

Word Wise

On page 183, the author uses the phrase "pretty well." This type of informal language helps give realistic fiction a conversational tone. Realistic fiction does not usually use the kind of formal language you would use in a research report.

Plan: Choose Your Topic

COLLABORATE

Brainstorm With a partner, talk about places you're interested in learning more about. The places must be or could be real. Then, on a sheet of paper, make a list of places and characters who either visit or live there. Brainstorm ideas of what the characters might do.

Writing Prompt Choose one place and some characters from your list. Decide who is your main character. Write a story about something interesting your character or characters discover about the place you chose. Remember stories usually have a conflict, or problem, that needs to be resolved.

I will write my story about _____

_____.

The main problem in the story is _____

_____.

Purpose and Audience Think about who will read or hear your story. Will your purpose be to inform, persuade, or entertain them? Then think about the language you will use to write your story.

My audience will be _____.

I will use _____ language when I write my story.

Plan In your writer's notebook, make a chart to plan the sequence of events in your story. Fill in the first event.

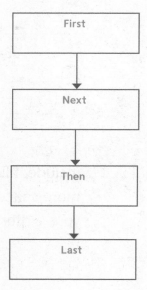

First

Next

Then

Last

Plan: Develop Characters

Brainstorm Details Once you have chosen your topic and decided on some details you plan to include, you will need to think carefully about your characters. Well-developed characters can make a story come to life in the readers' minds. As you write your first draft, ask yourself these questions:

- Have I described my characters' appearances?

- Have I thought carefully about my characters' personalities?

- How might I use more descriptive language to make a character more interesting?

- What do my characters want?

List two characters you might use in your story and describe them.

1 _____

_____

2 _____

_____

Graphic Organizer Once you've decided on all the characters you will include, fill in the rest of your Sequence of Events chart. If you need more space to write your details, use a separate sheet of paper in your writer's notebook.

Draft

Sequence A story has a beginning, a middle, and an end. Sequence is the order in which the plot events happen. Sometimes authors tell events out of order so that the reader can understand what happened in the past. In the example below from "Potluck or Potlatch," the events are told out of order, but the author uses "two weeks ago" to make the events clear.

> Alex exited the car and waved goodbye to his mother. Two weeks ago at the bus stop, Wakiash had given Alex a bundle of sticks wrapped in colorful ribbons strung with beads. Wakiash explained that his family was hosting a potluck in honor of his new baby sister, and the sticks were a traditional Native American invitation.

Now use the above paragraph as a model to write a paragraph that could go in your own story. Make sure the sequence of events is clear and that the events are realistic.

_____

_____

_____

_____

Write a Draft Use your Sequence of Events chart to help you write your draft in your writer's notebook. Remember to include dialogue and descriptive details. Check that your setting, or when and where the story takes place, is realistic.

Revise

Word Choice Effective writers choose their words carefully. They want to create a specific mood, or feeling, in their writing, and they choose the best words to support that mood. Read the passage below. Then revise it by adding descriptive language to more strongly create a happy mood.

> Anna was curious about the plaque in front of the telescope. She read it. Then she smiled and said, "Every month, they hold a star party where everyone gets to look through the telescope at night!"
> "That sounds like fun," Juan said.

Revision Revise your draft and think of the mood you are trying to create. Use descriptive words that will best help your reader visualize the mood and what is happening in the story.

Peer Conferences

COLLABORATE

Review a Draft Listen carefully as a partner reads his or her work aloud. Take notes about what you liked and what was difficult to follow. Begin by telling what you liked about the draft. Ask questions that will help the writer think more about the writing. Make suggestions that you think will make the writing stronger. Use these sentence starters.

I enjoyed this part of your draft because . . .

The sequence of events might be clearer if. . .

Try adding some descriptive words to help . . .

This part is unclear to me. Can you explain why . . . ?

Partner Feedback After your partner gives you feedback on your draft, write one of the suggestions that you will use in your revision. Refer to the rubric on page 31 as you give feedback.

Based on my partner's feedback, I will _____

_____

_____

_____

After you finish giving each other feedback, reflect on the peer conference. What was helpful? What might you do differently next time?

Revision As you revise your draft use the Revising Checklist to help you figure out what text you may need to move, elaborate on, or delete. Remember to use the rubric on page 31 to help you with your revision.

✓ Revising Checklist

- [ ] Does my writing fit my purpose and audience?
- [ ] Do my word choices contribute to the mood I want to create? Do I need to add, delete, or rearrange any words?
- [ ] Are all events presented in a logical order?
- [ ] Are the events realistic?
- [ ] Is there a conflict, or problem, in the story?
- [ ] Are the characters well developed? Do they talk and act like real people?

Edit and Proofread

When you **edit** and **proofread** your writing, you look for and correct mistakes in spelling, punctuation, capitalization, and grammar. Reading through a revised draft multiple times can help you make sure you're catching any errors. Use the checklist below to edit your story.

✔ Editing Checklist

- ☐ Do all sentences begin with a capital letter and end with a punctuation mark?
- ☐ Are there any run-on sentences or sentence fragments?
- ☐ Are all your action verbs used correctly?
- ☐ Are proper nouns capitalized?
- ☐ Are quotation marks used correctly?
- ☐ Are all words spelled correctly?

List two mistakes you found as you proofread your story.

1_____

_____

2_____

_____

Grammar Connection

When you write dialogue, make sure that everything characters say is in quotation marks. Use a comma to separate words such as *he said* from the quotation itself. For example:

He said, "I have soccer practice."

When a new character begins speaking, remember to begin a new line.

Publish, Present, and Evaluate

Publishing When you **publish** your writing, you create a clean, neat final copy that is free of mistakes. As you write your final draft be sure to write legibly in cursive. Check that you are holding your pencil or pen correctly and that you are spacing words correctly.

Presentation When you are ready to **present** your work, rehearse your presentation. Use the Presenting Checklist to help you.

Evaluate After you publish your writing, use the rubric below to **evaluate** your writing.

What did you do successfully? _____

What needs more work? _____

_____

Presenting Checklist

- ☐ Stand up straight.
- ☐ Look at the audience.
- ☐ Speak clearly and slowly.
- ☐ Speak loud enough so that everyone can hear you.
- ☐ Read with expression to help the audience understand how the characters feel and what is happening in the story.

4	3	2	1
• characters always act and speak like real people	• characters almost always act and speak like real people	• characters mostly do not act and speak like real people	• characters do not act and speak like real people
• settings are real or seem real	• most of the settings are real or seem real	• most of settings do not seem real	• settings are not realistic
• the events in the story could happen in real life	• most of the events in the story could happen in real life	• many of the events in the story could not happen in real life	• the events in the story could not happen in real life

Talk About It

Playing sports, building houses, or performing in a show are just some of the reasons people come together to work in teams. A group of artists collaborated on an art project for their community. They dedicated their time and talent to paint a mural.

Look at the photo. Talk with a partner about how you think working as a group benefits the artists and their community. Write the benefits in the web.

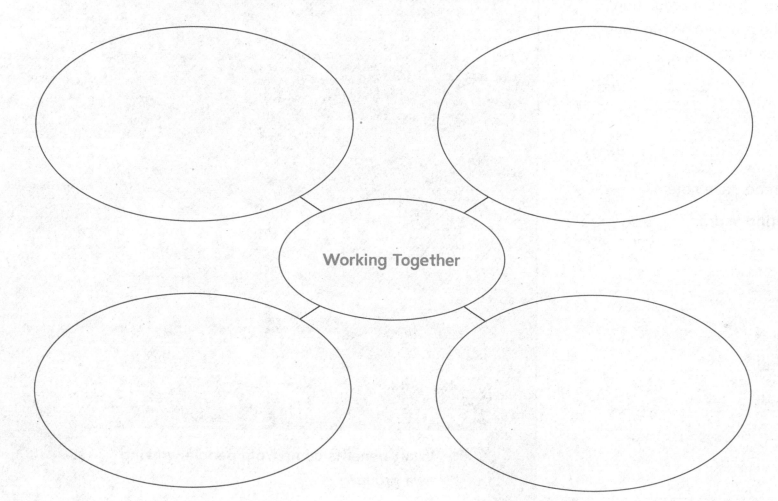

Working Together

Go online to **my.mheducation.com** and read the "Two Heads Are Better than One" Blast. Think about working together. When do you work on your own and when is it better to work as part of a team? Then blast back your response.

TAKE NOTES

Preview the text. Read the title, Essential Question, and first paragraph. Make a prediction about the problem. Write your prediction here.

_____

_____

_____

As you read, take note of:

Interesting Words _____

_____

_____

_____

Key Details _____

_____

_____

_____

_____

_____

Gulf Spill Superheroes

Essential Question

What benefits come from people working as a group?

Read about how a variety of people worked together after the Deepwater Horizon oil spill in the Gulf of Mexico.

Joe Raedle/Getty Images News/Getty Images

Fans of comic books know that sometimes it takes a team of superheroes to save the day. Each one uses his or her special powers to fight an enemy or solve a problem. On April 20, 2010, the Deepwater Horizon drilling platform exploded in the Gulf of Mexico. Massive fires raged above the waters. Down below, gallons and gallons of oil spewed from a broken pipeline. Such a huge disaster would require the skills and abilities of many heroes working together.

Fire boats at work at the off shore oil rig Deepwater Horizon.

Responders in the Water

Immediately after the explosion, firefighters worked with the U.S. Coast Guard to battle the blaze. Boats and aircraft transported survivors from the platform to safety before the rig sank.

Meanwhile, scientists raced to understand what was happening underwater. Each type of scientist had a specific **function.** Oceanographers mapped out the ocean floor and charted water currents in the area. Biologists looked for ways to protect animals in the region from the spreading oil.

What was most important, engineers discussed **techniques** to fix the broken well. The leak was more than a mile below the Gulf's surface. That was too deep for human divers to work effectively. For that reason, experts relied on robots with **artificial** arms and special tools to stop the spill. Many of their first efforts failed.

After nearly three months, workers finally plugged up the damaged well. It would take many more months to clean up the mess left behind.

◀ Workers move absorbent material to capture some spilled crude oil at Fourchon Beach, Louisiana.

(bkgd) Photodisc Collection/Eyewire/Getty Images; (tr) U.S. Coast Guard/Getty Images

FIND TEXT EVIDENCE

Read

Paragraph 1
Main Idea and Key Details

Look for details in paragraph 1. **Circle** the central, or main, idea in paragraph 1.

Paragraph 2
Latin Roots

The root *viv* means "to live." What is the meaning of *survivors* in paragraph 2?

_____

_____

Paragraphs 3-5
Ask and Answer Questions

How long did it take for the damaged well to be plugged up?

_____

Reread

Author's Craft

How does the author use descriptive language to help you picture the effects of the accident?

FIND TEXT EVIDENCE 🔍

Read

Paragraphs 1-2

Main Idea and Key Details

What is the central, or main, idea of "Watchers from the Sky"?

_____

_____

_____

Underline the text that supports the central idea.

Paragraphs 3-4

Ask and Answer Questions

Ask a question to check your understanding of "Heroes on Land."

_____

_____

Circle the answer to your question.

Reread

Author's Craft

How does the author help you understand the need for cooperation?

Watchers from the Sky

From the water, it was hard to see where the oil was spreading. Responders had to **collaborate** with other agencies, such as the NASA space program. Satellites in the sky sent information to scientists on the ground. Meteorologists tracked storms that might pose an **obstacle** to the response teams. Photographs helped team leaders decide how to assign their workers.

Pilots and their crews flew over the Gulf region in helicopters and planes. Some studied how the oil slick moved from place to place. Others directed the placement of floating barriers to protect sensitive areas. Some crews transferred needed supplies back and forth between land and sea.

Heroes on Land

As the oil approached land, new responders leapt into action. Veterinarians **dedicated** their efforts to helping out marine animals, such as pelicans and turtles. They would capture and treat affected animals before returning them to the wild. Naturalists and ecologists cleaned up the animals' habitats. Quite often, these groups' efforts overlapped and they helped one another. Volunteers also helped out on many tasks.

Local fishermen also needed help. They relied on crabs, shrimp, and other seafood for their livelihood. Government officials monitored fishing areas to decide which were safe. Bankers and insurance companies also reached out to the fishermen. They helped find ways to make up for the lost income from seafood sales.

Biologists catch an oil-soaked brown pelican to clean and return to the wild.

Saul Loeb/AFP/Getty Images

In Florida, experts worked together in a "think tank." They needed to trap floating globs of oil before they ruined area beaches. They created the SWORD, or Shallow-water Weathered Oil Recovery Device. The SWORD was a catamaran with mesh bags hung between its two pontoons. The small craft would **mimic** a pool skimmer and scoop up oil as it moved. Because of its size and speed, the SWORD could be quite **flexible** responding to spills.

Workers place absorbent materials to catch oil in Orange Beach, Alabama.

As we have seen, the Deepwater Horizon accident required heroic efforts of all kinds. In some cases, workers' jobs were quite distinct. In others, their goals and efforts were similar. The success of such a huge mission depended on how well these heroes worked together. The lessons learned will be quite valuable if and when another disaster happens.

(bkgd) Photodisc Collection/Eyewire/Getty Images; (tr) Joe Raedle/Getty Images News/Getty Images

Summarize

Use the subheads and your notes to write a summary about the Gulf oil spill. State the problem and the most important ideas used to solve it. Talk about whether your prediction on page 34 was correct.

FIND TEXT EVIDENCE 🔍

> Read

Paragraphs 1-2
Problem and Solution

Underline the problem mentioned in the first paragraph. How do the photo and caption work with the text to help you understand the solution to a problem?

_____

_____

_____

> Reread

Author's Craft

How does the author help you understand how the SWORD works?

Fluency

Take turns with a partner reading aloud the first paragraph on page 37. Discuss how you adjusted your reading rate or speed so you could read with accuracy.

Vocabulary

Use the example sentences to talk with a partner about each word. Then answer the questions.

artificial

Mike's **artificial** leg did not prevent him from playing most sports.

When might you want something to be artificial rather than real?

_____

_____

collaborate

Many students will **collaborate** to create our school's new banner.

What other projects might require you to collaborate with others?

_____

_____

dedicated

Tina **dedicated** herself to learning the song for the choir concert.

When have you dedicated all your efforts to learning something?

_____

_____

flexible

The dancer was so **flexible** that he could twist into almost any position.

Why is it important for athletes to be flexible?

_____

_____

function

The main **function** of a hammer is to pound nails.

What is the main function of another common tool?

_____

_____

Build Your Word List Reread the third paragraph on page 36. Circle the word _responders_. In your writer's notebook, use a word web to write more forms of the word. For example, write _responsive_. Use an online or print dictionary to find more words that are related and their definitions.

mimic

Some insects can **mimic** a twig to hide themselves.

What other animals can mimic something?

_____

_____

_____

obstacle

The fallen tree in the road was an **obstacle** for cars.

What sort of obstacle have you encountered trying to get somewhere?

_____

_____

_____

techniques

Maria uses a variety of bowing **techniques** when playing her violin.

What are some techniques you use to help you study?

_____

_____

(l) Photodisc Collection/Eyewire/Getty Images; (r) Saul Loeb/AFP/Getty Images

Latin Roots

A root can be a clue to the meaning of an unfamiliar word. Some roots from ancient Latin are *sensus*, which means "perceive" or "feel"; *habitare*, which means "to live" or "to dwell"; and *port*, which means "carry." The prefix *trans-*, which means "across," also comes from ancient Latin.

FIND TEXT EVIDENCE

I know that the Latin root mare *means "the ocean or sea." Other context clues talk about how the oil spill affected life, so I can figure out that* marine *means "of or relating to the sea."*

> Veterinarians dedicated their efforts to helping out marine animals, such as pelicans and turtles.

Your Turn Use your knowledge of Latin roots to figure out the meanings of the following words from "Gulf Spill Superheroes":

transported, page 35 _____

sensitive, page 36 _____

habitats, page 36 _____

_____

Ask and Answer Questions

As you read an article, you may need to make adjustments when you do not understand some details. As you read "Gulf Spill Superheroes," you can stop, ask questions, and then look for answers.

🔍 FIND TEXT EVIDENCE

When you read "Watchers from the Sky" on page 36, you may get confused about how pilots and their crews helped. Ask, *Why would pilots and their crews be in charge of where to place floating barriers?* Then reread to find the answer.

Page 36

Watchers from the Sky

From the water, it was hard to see where the oil was spreading. Responders had to **collaborate** with other agencies, such as the NASA space program. Satellites in the sky sent information to scientists on the ground. Meteorologists tracked storms that might pose an **obstacle** to the response teams. Photographs helped team leaders decide how to assign their workers.

Pilots and their crews flew over the Gulf region in helicopters and planes. Some studied how the oil slick moved from place to place. Others directed the placement of floating barriers to protect sensitive areas. Some crews transferred needed supplies back and forth between land and sea.

I reread the beginning of the section: From the water, it was hard to see where the oil was spreading. *People placing the floating barriers needed pilots above to see the oil, so pilots were in charge.*

Your Turn Ask and answer a question about the information in "Responders in the Water" on page 35. As you read, use the strategy Ask and Answer Questions.

_____

_____

_____

_____

Problem and Solution

"Gulf Spill Superheroes" is expository text. Expository text gives factual information about a topic and may use a problem-and-solution text structure. The author may offer conclusions supported by evidence. Expository text may also include print and graphic features such as photographs, captions, and headings. These make a text multimodal.

FIND TEXT EVIDENCE

I can tell that "Gulf Spill Superheroes" is expository text about the Gulf Spill responders. The author uses a problem-and-solution text structure by telling the problem and describing solutions. Headings help organize the text. Photographs and captions provide additional information.

Page 36

Watchers from the Sky

From the water, it was hard to see where the oil was spreading. Responders had to **collaborate** with other agencies, such as the NASA space program. Satellites in the sky sent information to scientists on the ground. Meteorologists tracked storms that might pose an **obstacle** to the response teams. Photographs helped team leaders decide how to assign their workers.

Pilots and their crews flew over the Gulf region in helicopters and planes. Some studied how the oil slick moved from place to place. Others directed the placement of floating barriers to protect sensitive areas. Some crews transferred needed supplies back and forth between land and sea.

Heroes on Land

As the oil approached land, new responders leapt into action. Veterinarians **dedicated** their efforts to helping out marine animals, such as pelicans and turtles. They would capture and treat affected animals before returning them to the wild. Naturalists and ecologists cleaned up the animals' habitats. Quite often, these groups' efforts overlapped and they helped one another. Volunteers also helped out on many tasks.

Local fishermen also needed help. They relied on crabs, shrimp, and other seafood for their livelihood. Government officials monitored fishing areas to decide which were safe. Bankers and insurance companies also reached out to the fishermen. They helped find ways to make up for the lost income from seafood sales.

Biologists catch an oil-soaked brown pelican to clean and return to the wild.

Saul Loeb/AFP/Getty Images

Photographs and Captions

Photographs help to illustrate the information in the text. Captions provide additional information.

COLLABORATE

Your Turn List an example of information that the author includes that shows problem-and-solution text structure. How do the photograph and caption on page 36 add details to the text?

_____

_____

_____

_____

Main Idea and Key Details

The **main idea**, or central idea, of an article is what it is mostly about. Each section and paragraph in an article also has a main idea. A main idea is supported by evidence, such as facts and key details. To find the main idea, identify **key details** and figure out what they have in common.

Quick Tip

Sometimes headings give a clue to the main, or central, idea. List the key details that support the heading. Then determine, or decide, what the details have in common.

🔍 FIND TEXT EVIDENCE

When I read the section "Heroes on Land" on page 36, I see that all the details are arranged about the efforts of people on land working to help others. From this I can find the main idea.

Main Idea
As the oil spill reached land, other responders went to work.
Detail
Veterinarians and naturalists helped animals affected by the oil.
Detail
Business leaders helped fishermen who could not fish in some areas.
Detail
Members of a "think tank" created the SWORD to protect local beaches.

 Your Turn Reread "Responders in the Water" on page 35. Use the graphic organizer on page 43 to record text evidence about how responders helped to deal with the disaster.

Main Idea
Detail
Detail
Detail

Respond to Reading

COLLABORATE

Discuss the prompt below. Think about how the author focuses on how people responded to the Gulf oil spill. Use your notes and graphic organizer to write a brief composition that answers the question below.

How does the author help you understand that it took a team of people to help with the Deepwater Horizon accident?

_____

_____

_____

_____

_____

_____

_____

_____

_____

_____

_____

_____

_____

Quick Tip

Use these sentence starters to discuss the text and to organize ideas.

- *The headings tell...*
- *The author gives specific ideas...*
- *Problems were solved by...*

Grammar Connections

Check that you have correctly punctuated compound sentences. A compound sentence contains two simple sentences joined together by a comma and a conjunction. For example, *They saw a problem, and they wanted to help.* Conjunctions include *and, but,* and *or.*

Generate and Clarify Questions

A good way to focus research is to **generate and clarify questions.**
Think of questions you want to answer with research. Clarifying
questions help you understand confusing or complex ideas.

- When asking a person to clarify what they are saying, you may ask,
  "What did you mean. . . ? Can you tell me more about. . . ?"
- You can also ask yourself "What does this mean?" about
  information you read. Be specific about what you need to know.

After you ask a clarifying question about your research on a topic, what

would you do to find an answer? _____

_____

_____

Create a Television Segment With a group, research a rescue group
that helps animals. Then create a television segment that explores what
the group does to help animals survive in their own ecosystems.

Discuss the questions you want answered in your research. Plan the
audio pieces, photos, and videos you can include in your multimodal
presentation. Members of your group might play the parts of people
from the rescue group to give information and answer questions. One
student should be the director. This student should give oral instructions
such as where to stand or who speaks in which order.

After you complete your television segment, you will be presenting your
work to your class.

Quick Tip

You can generate and
clarify questions for formal
inquiry or informal inquiry.
Formal inquiry means
using sources such as
books, magazines, or
websites to look for
information. Informal
inquiry means talking to
people you know to get
information.

Generate question:

- How does the group
  help animals?

Clarify question:

- Why do the animals
  need help?

What other clarifying
question might you ask?

_____

_____

_____

Literature Anthology:
pages 198–211

Winter's Tail

? **How do you know that the aquarium staff is concerned about Winter?**

Talk About It Reread paragraphs 2 and 3 on **Literature Anthology** page 202. Look at the photograph. Talk with a partner about how the staff helps Winter when she arrives at the aquarium.

Cite Text Evidence What evidence shows how the trainers feel about Winter? Write it in the chart.

Text Evidence	Photograph Clues	What It Shows

Quick Tip

Focus on the details about the aquarium staff. Pay attention to descriptive words about their actions.

Write I know that the aquarium staff is concerned about Winter because the authors _____

_____

_____

? **How do the authors help you visualize what the team had to think about while creating Winter's prosthesis?**

COLLABORATE

Talk About It Reread the last paragraph on **Literature Anthology** page 207. Turn to a partner and talk about what the team had to consider as they created the prosthesis.

Cite Text Evidence What words and phrases help you create a mental image of what the team did? Write text evidence in the chart.

Text Evidence	What I Visualize

Synthesize Information

How can looking up the definitions of unfamiliar science terms help you better visualize the text? Use an online source to find the definitions of *prosthesis* and *mimic*. Consider those definitions when visualizing the teams efforts.

Write I can visualize how the team created the prosthesis because

the author _____

? **How do the authors show how Winter will continue to have an impact on the people who helped her?**

Talk About It Reread the second paragraph on **Literature Anthology** page 211. Turn to a partner and discuss what the team will need to do.

Cite Text Evidence What does the team need to do in order to continue to help Winter? What is their goal? Write text evidence in the chart.

Text Evidence

↓

Text Evidence

↓

What I Know

Write I know that Winter will continue to be a part of her team's lives because _____

_____

_____

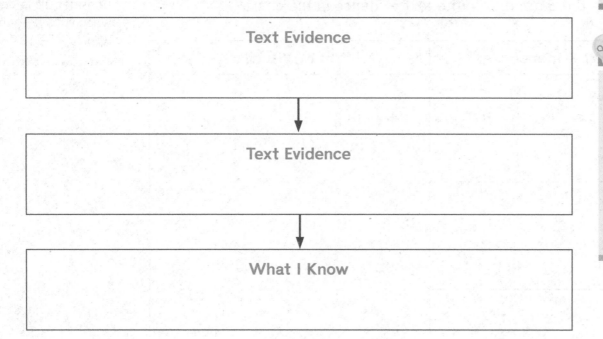

Respond to Reading

COLLABORATE

Discuss the prompt below. Apply your own experiences with animals or stories about people who have been involved with animals to inform your answer. Use your notes and graphic organizer.

How do the authors help you understand how many people have been inspired by Winter's story?

_____

_____

_____

_____

_____

_____

_____

_____

_____

_____

_____

Self-Selected Reading

Choose a text and fill in your writer's notebook with the title, author, and genre. Record your purpose for reading. For example, you may be reading to answer a question or for entertainment.

Rene Frederic/age fotostock

Helping Hands

Literature Anthology:
pages 214-217

A Need Inspires

1   The rules of the competition asked participants to come up with new and innovative ways to help heal, repair or improve the human body. One of the group members, Kate Murray, understood the difficulties people with an injury or impairment can face. Kate was born with a left hand that was not fully formed. But that didn't stop Kate from taking part in activities. When she decided she wanted to learn how to play the violin, she and her mother worked with a team of specialists to create a device to allow her to hold a bow.

2   The Flying Monkeys wondered if they could create something similar for the competition. When one of their Girl Scouts coaches learned about Danielle Fairchild, a three-year-old who was born without fingers on her right hand, the Flying Monkeys found their inspiration.

Reread paragraph 1. **Underline** why Kate Murray understands how people with an injury or impairment feel.

Circle clues that help you understand what Kate is like.

COLLABORATE

Reread paragraph 2. Talk with a partner about how the Flying Monkeys found their inspiration. **Make a mark** in the margin beside the text evidence.

Why is "A Need Inspires" a good heading for this section? Use text evidence to write your answer here:

_____

_____

Introducing the BOB-1

[1]   Before long, the Flying Monkeys settled on a final design for their invention, which they called the BOB-1. They used a flexible plastic substance, a pencil grip, and hook-and-eye closures to build it. Everyone involved was impressed by how well the device would fit on Danielle's hand. What's more, it was very simple and inexpensive to make. Why hadn't anyone thought of creating a device like this before?

[2]   The Flying Monkeys created fliers, a portfolio, and even a skit to take to the competition and showcase their invention. The competition judges were impressed.

[3]   The Flying Monkeys won a regional and state-level innovation award. From there, it was on to the global round of the contest, where the BOB-1 would be judged alongside 178 other entries from 16 countries. The winning team would receive $20,000 to further develop the product.

In paragraph 1, **underline** how the author describes the BOB-1.

Reread paragraph 2. **Circle** what the group did to impress the judges at the competition. Write text evidence here:

1. _____

2. _____

3. _____

COLLABORATE

Reread paragraph 3. Talk about what happened at the competition and where the Flying Monkeys were headed next. **Draw a box** around how the author helps you understand the word *global*.

? **How does the author organize the information to help you understand what the Flying Monkeys did to create BOB-1?**

Talk About It Look back at your text evidence and annotations on pages 50–51. With a partner, talk about how the author organizes the information to help you understand what the Flying Monkeys do.

Cite Text Evidence What are the ways the author organizes the text? Write them here.

How the Author Organizes the Text

Write I use the way the author organizes information to help me understand _____

_____

_____

_____

ktaylorg/iStock/Getty Images

Literal and Figurative Language

To describe something, an author can use literal or figurative language. Literal language means exactly what it says. In figurative language, words are used in a different way from their usual meaning. Figurative language can be used to help readers better visualize something.

FIND TEXT EVIDENCE

In "Helping Hands" on **Literature Anthology** page 215, the author uses "cast aside" to describe what happened to "old ideas." The Flying Monkeys did not literally, or actually, throw an idea away. The author used "cast aside" to help readers visualize the process of finding an idea that works.

> Old ideas were cast aside and new ideas began to take shape.

Your Turn Reread the first paragraph under "Introducing the BOB-1" on page 51.

• What descriptive words does the author use to help you visualize the device the Flying Monkeys invented? _____

_____

• Why do you think the author used literal instead of figurative language to describe the device? _____

_____

_____

Think about the words you choose. Ask yourself whether literal or figurative language will be better to help readers visualize the meaning of your text. Here is an example of literal language: *The team was inspired to invent something.* Here is the same thought using figurative language: *Inspiration struck the team like lightning.*

Text Connections

? **How do advances in technology allow these firefighters and the teams described in *Winter's Tail* and "Helping Hands" to help others?**

Talk About It Look at the lithograph. Read the caption. The water pumps in the picture are steam powered. This was new technology at the time. Talk with a partner about what the firefighters are doing.

Cite Text Evidence **Draw a box** around the details that show the water pumps are steam powered. **Circle** as many different jobs you see the firefighters doing.

Write I see how advances in technology helps others _____

_____

_____

_____

_____

_____

_____

_____

_____

Library of Congress Prints and Photographs Division ILC-DIG-pga-008II]

The Life of a Fireman: The New Era. Steam and Muscle was created in 1861 by American illustrator Charles Parsons. It was printed by Currier & Ives.

Present Your Work

COLLABORATE

Discuss how you will present your television segment on an animal rescue group. Perhaps you will decide to present to a live audience, your class. Use the Presenting Checklist as you practice your presentation. Discuss the sentence starters below and write your answers.

In my research about an animal rescue group, I was most interested in

_____

_____

_____

I would like to research more about _____

_____

_____

_____

Tech Tip

If you use videos and photos from a website, tell your audience the source of your information. Also, check that the recording equipment is set up correctly and working.

✓ Presenting Checklist

☐ Plan with your group how you will present your television segment, including the audio and visual parts.

☐ Rehearse your presentation. The director should give oral instructions that include multiple action steps.

☐ Use natural gestures when you speak.

☐ Allow time for questions. Provide complete answers.

Sandy Watt/Alamy Stock Photo

Talk About It

Essential Question

How do we explain what happened in the past?

Artifacts are remnants of the past. They help us understand how people lived. Artifacts can be unearthed all over the world. When they are found, they may not always be in one piece.

Look at the photo. What is the woman doing? Talk with a partner and discuss how the woman can learn about what happened in the past by examining and reconstructing artifacts. Write ways you can learn about the past in the web.

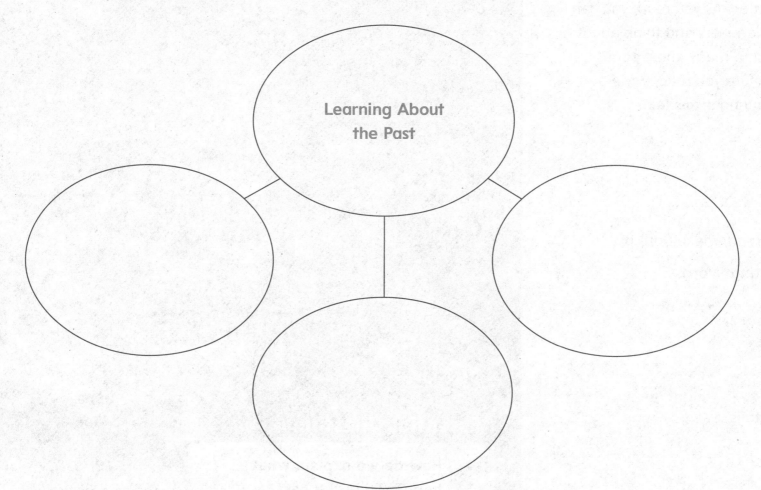

Learning About
the Past

Go online to **my.mheducation.com** and read the "Remnants of the Past" Blast. Think about the statues that were found. How does studying them help us learn about the past? Then blast back your response.

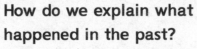

TAKE NOTES

Asking questions about a text helps you decide on a purpose for reading, such as reading to gain information. As you read, you can look for answers and think about what you already know about a topic. Before you read, write a question about this text.

_____

_____

_____

As you read, make note of:

Interesting Words _____

_____

_____

_____

Key Details _____

_____

_____

_____

Essential Question

How do we explain what happened in the past?

Read two different views about the uses of a fascinating object.

The Inca Empire was centered in what is now Peru. It was taken by Spanish conquest in the middle of the 16th century.

What Was the Purpose of the Inca's KNOTTED STRINGS?

POINT COUNTERPOINT

String Theory

Was the quipu an ancient mathematical calculator?

Most of us do not do math problems without an electronic calculator. It would be even tougher without paper and pencil. Now imagine adding numbers with a device full of knotted strings! The quipu (pronounced KWEE-poo) was an invention of the Incas, an ancient civilization in South America. Most quipus were not **preserved**, but about 600 of them still remain **intact**.

Quipus are made of cotton and wool strings, sometimes hundreds of them, attached to a thicker horizontal cord. Both the **archaeologist** and the **historian** have tried to figure out how the quipu works. Here is their solution:

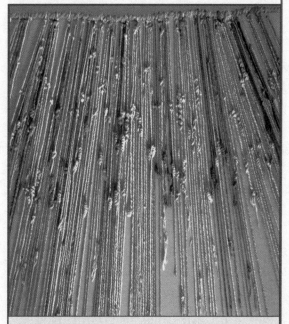

The quipu is an object that has baffled archaeologists for many years.

Knots were tied to the dangling strings to represent numbers.

The quipus were likely used by Inca officials to record and keep track of data, including statistics on anything from the number of crops produced by a village to the number of people living in a house.

FIND TEXT EVIDENCE 🔍

Read

Paragraphs 1–2
Summarize

Underline the key idea you would use in a summary of the first two paragraphs. Write it here.

Paragraph 3
Context Clues

Circle the words that help you determine the meaning of *statistics*. Write the meaning here.

Make Inferences

Why might officials have wanted to record the number of crops and people in a village?

Reread

Author's Craft

How does the author help you understand what a quipu looks like?

SHARED READ

FIND TEXT EVIDENCE

Read

Paragraphs 1–2

Author's Point of View

Underline the sentence that states the first author's claim about the quipu. Discuss why a quipu was amazing.

_____

_____

Paragraphs 3–4

Summarize

What key idea would connect the first two paragraphs in a summary of "Spinning a Yarn"?

_____

_____

_____

_____

Reree

Author's Craft

How does the author of "Spinning a Yarn" help you understand why the ancient Incas are so fascinating?

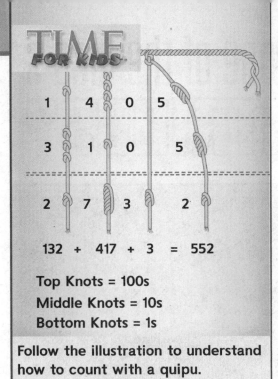

1	4	0	5
3	1	0	5
2	7	3	2

132 + 417 + 3 = 552

Top Knots = 100s
Middle Knots = 10s
Bottom Knots = 1s

Follow the illustration to understand how to count with a quipu.

Here is how a quipu would work: Each group of knots on a string represents a power of 10. Depending on their position, knots can stand for ones, tens, hundreds, and thousands. Clusters of knots increase in value the higher they are on the string. As a result, Incas with special training could add up the knots on a string to get the sum. They could also add up the total of many strings or even many quipus.

The patterns of the knots show repeating numbers. When you add it all up, it seems clear that the quipu was nothing less than an amazing low-tech calculator.

COUNTERPOINT

Spinning a Yarn

The Incas had a 3-D language written in thread!

Questions surround the Inca civilization. In its peak **era**—the middle of the 1400s—the Incas built thousands of miles of roads over mountains, and yet they didn't have wheeled vehicles. They made houses of stone blocks that fit together perfectly without mortar, a bonding material. The biggest question may be how the Incas kept their empire together without a written language.

The answer to the last question might be an odd-looking object called a quipu. Only a few hundred of these **remnants** of the Inca culture still exist.

Researchers discuss a quipu.

(t) Neil Stewart; (b) STR/AP Images

Quipus are made of wool strings that hang from a thick cord. On the strings are groups of knots. Many researchers believe the knots stand for numbers—even though no evidence supports this. But others make a strong case that the knots of the quipu were really language symbols, or a form of language.

Researchers found an identical three-knot pattern in the strings of seven different quipus. They think the order of the knots is code for the name of an Incan city. They hope to **reconstruct** the quipu code based on this and other repeating patterns of knots.

More conclusive proof that the quipu is a language comes from an old manuscript, a series of handwritten pages from the 17th century. It was found in a box holding **fragments** of a quipu. The author of the manuscript says the quipus were woven symbols. The manuscript even matches up the symbols to a list of words.

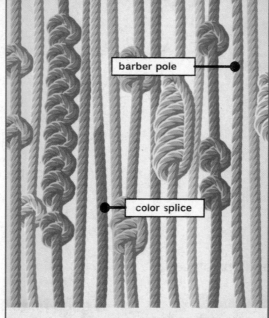

barber pole

color splice

Some experts now believe that the quipu's knots, colors, and patterns made it more than just a counting device. Decoding the quipu may reveal historical records.

The Inca empire covered nearly 3,000 miles. Perhaps the strings of the quipu helped hold it together.

Summarize

Use your notes, the diagram, and the illustration to orally summarize the two different points of view about the Incan quipu.

FIND TEXT EVIDENCE 🔍

Read

Paragraphs 1–4

Author's Point of View

Draw a box around the author's claim about quipus in the first paragraph.

Underline the evidence that supports this claim.

Diagrams

Circle information under the illustration that suggests an explanation for the quipu's knots. What does the illustration suggest?

_____

_____

Reread

Author's Craft

How does the illustration support the author's claim?

Neil Stewart

Vocabulary

Use the example sentences to talk with a partner about each word. Then answer the questions.

archaeologist

An **archaeologist** looks for clues about ancient places and early cultures.

What ancient place would you visit if you were an archaeologist?

_____

_____

era

The people in the photograph wore clothes from an earlier **era**.

If you could time travel to a different era, which would you choose?

_____

_____

fragments

The vase was in **fragments** after it fell on the floor.

What fragments of objects have you found?

_____

_____

historian

A good **historian** finds interesting stories by studying past objects and events.

What would a future historian tell about the time you live in?

_____

_____

intact

Cardboard cartons help protect eggs and keep them **intact**.

What would you like to find intact after a storm?

_____

_____

Build Your Word List Pick a word you found interesting in the selection you read. Look up the definition in a print or online dictionary. Write the word and its definition in your writer's notebook.

preserved

We **preserved** food from our garden in jars.

Which of your possessions would you want preserved in a time capsule?

_____

_____

reconstruct

We had to **reconstruct** our snow fort after it fell apart.

What things have you had to reconstruct?

_____

_____

remnants

Divers discovered the **remnants** of a sunken ship.

What could someone learn from the remnants of a meal?

_____

_____

Context Clues

When you come across an unfamiliar or multiple-meaning word, context clues found in the same sentence may help you determine its meaning. Sentence clues are words or phrases that help support the meaning of an unfamiliar word.

🔍 FIND TEXT EVIDENCE

In the first paragraph of "String Theory," I do not know the meaning of calculator. _The words_ do math problems _and_ electronic _in the sentence suggest that a calculator is a computer that solves math problems._

Most of us do not do math problems without an electronic calculator. It would be even tougher without paper and pencil.

Your Turn Use sentence clues to figure out the meanings of the following words from "String Theory" and "Spinning a Yarn."

patterns, *page 60* _____

manuscript, *page 61* _____

_____

Summarize

Summarizing argumentative texts as you read is a good way to keep track of how the authors make important points. Summarize sections as you read and then summarize the whole text to check your understanding.

🔍 **FIND TEXT EVIDENCE**

As you read "String Theory" on pages 59 and 60, summarize the author's theory of how the quipu might have been used.

Page 60

Here is how a quipu would work: Each group of knots on a string represents a power of 10. Depending on their position, knots can stand for ones, tens, hundreds, and thousands. Clusters of knots increase in value the higher they are on the string. As a result, Incas with special training could add up the knots on a string to get the sum. They could also add up the total of many strings or even many quipus.

The Incas' quipu had different patterns of knots on strings. Experts think the quipu may have been a calculator, and the patterns may have stood for numbers of different values.

> **Quick Tip**
>
> A summary is a short retelling of a text. When you summarize an argumentative text, you state the author's claim and the most important details that support the claim.

Your Turn Identify and summarize the claim in "Spinning a Yarn."

_____

_____

_____

Compare and Contrast

An argumentative text tries to persuade an intended audience to support a claim supported with facts. You can **compare** and **contrast** two argumentative texts by seeing what is similar and different. For example, the authors of "String Theory" and "Spinning a Yarn" both think the quipu's knots have meaning, but each author has a different idea about that meaning. The texts also include diagrams that you can compare and contrast.

FIND TEXT EVIDENCE

I can tell that "String Theory" is argumentative text because it states a claim of how a quipu may have been used. Details about how the quipu worked support the claim. A diagram illustrates the information.

Page 60

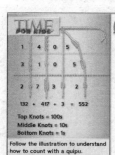

Diagram

A diagram is a simple visual representation of an object, place, idea, or event. Labels show how parts relate to one another and to the whole.

Your Turn How does the diagram on page 60 contrast with the diagram on page 61?

_____

_____

_____

_____

Author's Point of View

When an author of an argumentative text argues for or against an idea, the author gives his or her point of view, or claim, about the topic. Supporting details such as word choice, evidence, and reasons for or against an argument give readers clues about the author's point of view.

🔍 FIND TEXT EVIDENCE

I will read "Spinning a Yarn" to look for evidence of the author's point of view. Just below the title is this sentence: The Incas had a 3-D language written in thread! *It shows that the author supports a connection between the quipu and language. The author provides evidence to support the idea that the knots were not counting devices but were language symbols.*

Details	Author's Point of View
"Incas had a language in thread."	The author is in favor of quipu as a form of language.
knots may not mean numbers	
patterns may be symbols	
old manuscript shows a code	

Your Turn Identify important details in "String Theory" and place them in your graphic organizer on page 67. Then state the author's point of view.

Details	Author's Point of View

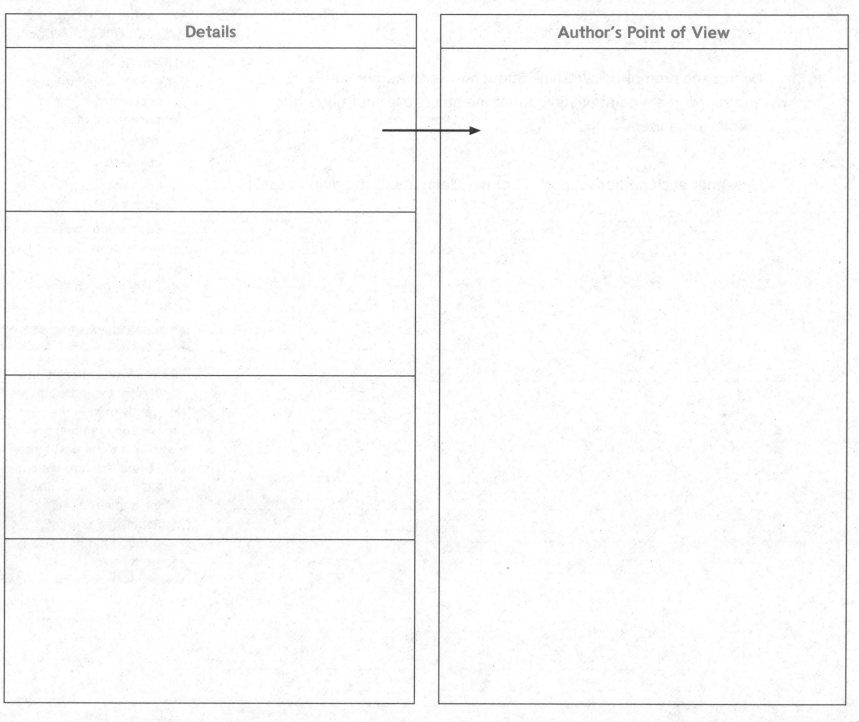

Respond to Reading

COLLABORATE

Discuss the prompt below. Think about how each author stated and supported a point of view about the quipu. Use your notes and graphic organizer.

How does each author support his or her claim about the quipu's use?

_____

_____

_____

_____

_____

_____

_____

_____

_____

_____

_____

_____

_____

_____

_____

Audio and Visual Features

Audio and visual features can enhance a research project. Audio features include music, recorded speeches, or recorded sounds from places and events. Visual features include videos, photos, diagrams, or graphs. When choosing features, ask

- What parts of the project would be more effective with a visual or audio feature?
- Does the feature focus on the topic or is it just a decoration?

What would you look for when selecting audio or visual features?

_____

_____

The Ancestral Puebloans built and lived in large communities like these cliff dwellings. What does the photograph show that would be hard to describe in words?

_____

_____

_____

Research Presentation With a partner or in a group, research details about the ancestors of a Native American civilization. Think about how to present the information. Select a genre, for example, an opinion essay, a speech, or a poem, for your topic and intended audience. Then plan a first draft by brainstorming, mapping, or freewriting your ideas. Think about features you might include. For example

- Are there photographs of sites where the people lived or artifacts they used?
- Are there recordings of someone speaking the language?

Then plan your presentation and write and revise your information. After you complete your piece, you will be sharing your work with the class. Be sure to include information that will interest your classmates and teacher.

Machu Picchu: Ancient City

? **How does the author organize the information to help you understand his or her point of view?**

Literature Anthology: pages 218–221

COLLABORATE

Talk About It Reread "A Reasonable Retreat" on **Literature Anthology** page 219. Turn to your partner and talk about how the author builds information to support his or her opinion.

Cite Text Evidence What words and phrases does the author use to organize the information? Write text evidence in the chart.

Text Evidence

Point of View

Make Inferences

Sometimes authors do not explain everything on the page. The author writes that archaeologists have tried to figure out why the Incas built Machu Picchu where it is. What inference can you make about Machu Picchu's location?

Write The author organizes his or her point of view by

_____

_____

? **How does the author use literal language to help you visualize the Temple of the Sun?**

COLLABORATE

Talk About It Reread the fourth paragraph on **Literature Anthology** page 220. Turn to your partner and describe what the Temple of the Sun is like.

Cite Text Evidence What words and phrases help you visualize what the Temple of the Sun looks like? Write text evidence in the chart.

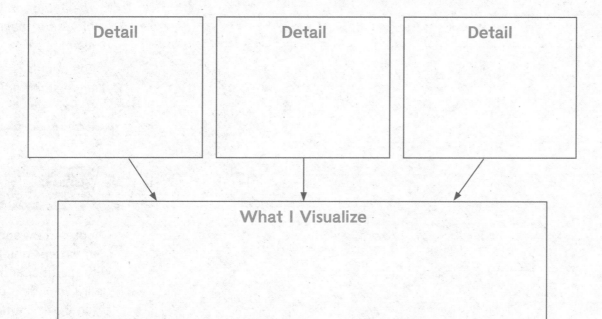

Detail	Detail	Detail

What I Visualize

Write The author uses literal language to help me visualize the Temple of the Sun by _____

_____

_____

_____

Respond to Reading

Discuss the prompt below. Think about the details in both argumentative texts and how the authors support their points of view to inform your answer. Use your notes and graphic organizer.

How do the authors use details to support their positions?

_____

_____

_____

_____

_____

_____

_____

_____

_____

_____

_____

_____

_____

_____

Jindrich Kolar/Shutterstock.com

Dig This Technology!

1. Another tool archaeologists use is a device that looks like a lawn mower. Called "ground penetrating radar" (GPR), it uses radar to locate artifacts under the ground. Radar bounces radio waves off an object to show its location. The diagram below shows how GPR helps archaeologists find artifacts.

Ground Penetrating Radar

One antenna sends radio waves into the ground. The other antenna receives waves when they bounce back. A wave that hits an object bounces back at a different depth than other waves. The depths are plotted on a display screen, revealing buried objects.

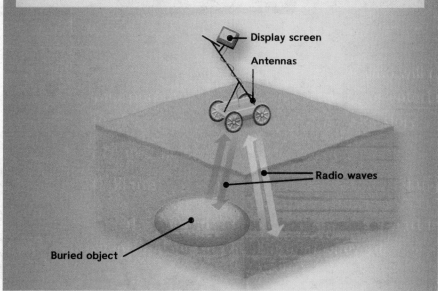

Display screen

Antennas

Radio waves

Buried object

Literature Anthology: pages 222–223

Reread paragraph 1. **Circle** how the author describes the ground penetrating radar to help you understand what it looks like. **Underline** what the GPR does.

COLLABORATE

Look at the diagram. Talk with a partner about what the caption describes and what you see in the diagram. How does this help you understand more about what the GPR does? Use text evidence to write your response here:

_____

_____

_____

_____

_____

_____

? How does the diagram help you understand how scientists find and analyze artifacts?

Talk About It Reread the excerpt on page 73 and look at the diagram. With a partner, talk about what the diagram shows.

Cite Text Evidence What clues in the diagram help you understand how it helps scientists find and analyze buried artifacts? Write evidence in the chart.

Quick Tip

As you read each sentence in the caption, refer to the part of the diagram the sentence explains.

Evidence	How It Helps

Write The diagram helps me understand _____

_____

_____

_____

Figurative Language

Writers use **figurative language** to help readers create mental images to deepen understanding or to make a strong point. Figurative language has a different meaning from the actual, literal, meaning of the words used.

FIND TEXT EVIDENCE

In "Dig This Technology!" on page 223 of the **Literature Anthology,** the author creates a word picture to make a strong point about why new technology is helpful to archaeologists. The language used does not mean that archaeologists literally dig. It means they can look into the past with new ways today.

> Now, archaeologists can dig into the past, without having to lift a shovel.

Your Turn Read the following sentence:
Archaeologists use many different tools to carefully remove layers of dirt to find items people left in the ground long ago.

- Use figurative language to rewrite the sentence.

_____

_____

- Why did you choose to use this language?

_____

_____

Use figurative language in your writing to help readers create mental images of what you are describing. For example, if you want to describe the size of a large stone, you may write, "The stone was as big as an elephant."

Text Connections

? How do the photographer and the authors of *Machu Picchu: Ancient City* and "Dig This Technology!" help you understand how people learn about the past by reconstructing and researching it?

Talk About It Look at the photograph. Read the caption. Talk with a partner about what the paleontologist is doing.

COLLABORATE

Cite Text Evidence **Draw a box** around clues in the photograph that show what Dr. Ross is doing. **Circle** some of the things he does to recreate the skeleton. In the caption, **underline** text evidence that explains what he is preparing the skeleton for.

Write I understand how reconstructing and researching the past helps people learn more because _____

_____

_____

_____

_____

_____

_____

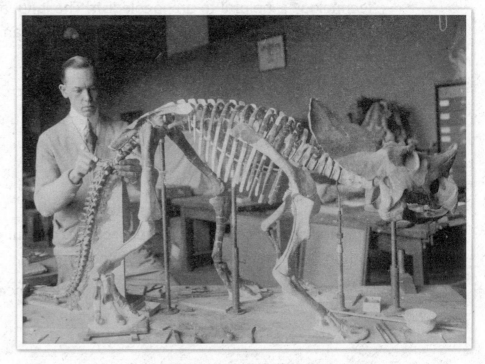

Norman Ross, a paleontologist, prepares a skeleton of a baby dinosaur for an exhibit. Ross worked at the National Museum in 1921.

Accuracy and Rate

To read argumentative text with **accuracy**, make sure that you pronounce each word and number correctly. You may need to adjust your **rate**, or speed, to read more slowly so that the words are clear and correct.

Page 60

Questions surround the Inca civilization. In its peak era—the middle of the 1400s—the Incas built thousands of miles of roads over mountains, and yet they didn't have wheeled vehicles.

Think about how you would read years in contrast to how you would read other numbers.

Think about how you would use punctuation to adjust your rate.

Quick Tip

Preview the text before you read aloud. Look for special words and words with multiple syllables. Note punctuation. Then plan your reading rate.

Your Turn Turn to page 61. Take turns reading aloud the third paragraph with a partner. Think about how to read the number and specialized words such as *quipu*. Plan your rate of reading so that you can read with accuracy.

Afterward, think about how you did. Complete these sentences.

I remembered to _____

_____

Next time I will _____

_____

Expert Model

Literature Anthology: pages 218–221

Features of a Persuasive Article

A persuasive article is a form of argumentative text. It presents a viewpoint about a topic. A persuasive article

- clearly expresses the author's claim

- supports the argument with facts and details in a logical order

- uses precise language to connect ideas

Analyze an Expert Model Studying argumentative texts will help you learn how to plan and write a persuasive article. **Reread** "A Reasonable Retreat" on page 219 in the **Literature Anthology.** Write your answers to the questions below.

How does the author express his or her claim? _____

_____

_____

_____

How does the author support his or her claim? _____

_____

_____

_____

Word Wise

On page 219, the author uses the phrase "Given this evidence . . ." This type of language helps to give your writing a more formal tone. It can also help the reader understand your opinion about the topic in a persuasive article.

Plan: Choose Your Topic

Brainstorm With a partner, brainstorm a list of ancient sites that have left people with unanswered questions. For example, there are many unanswered questions about the pyramids in Egypt. Search some websites for more ideas. Write your list on the lines below.

_____

_____

_____

Writing Prompt Choose one ancient site from your list. Then, read more about it. Choose the argument you think is the most likely explanation for the site. Write a persuasive article that includes differing points of view. Then, convince readers that one argument is more likely than the other.

I will write about _____.

Purpose and Audience Think about who will read or hear your article. Then, think about the language you will use to write your article.

My audience will be _____.

I will use _____ language when I write my article.

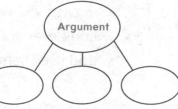

Argument

Plan In your writer's notebook, make a web to plan your writing. Fill in the argument.

Plan: Specific Facts and Details

Support an Argument Once you have chosen an ancient site to write about and a likely explanation for the unanswered question, you will need to research another explanation to address and refute. It is important to record in your writer's notebook convincing, specific facts from your research. As you plan your first draft, ask

- Have I done enough research related specifically to my topic?

- Have I thought carefully about the explanation that is the most likely?

- Do I have enough supporting facts and details to make my argument convincing and to argue against another explanation?

List two facts that you will use in your article.

1 _____

2 _____

Take Notes As you do your research, check that you have correctly copied any quotes you plan to use. Keep track of your sources in case you need to refer to them again and for when you cite them. Look over your notes, choose the facts that best support the argument, and use them to fill in your web.

> **Digital Tools**
>
> For more information on how to take notes, watch the "Take Notes: Print" video. Go to **my.mheducation.com.**

Draft

Logical Order Authors of persuasive articles want to convince an audience, so they carefully consider their introductions, transitions, and conclusions. Evidence should be presented in logical order. Authors may choose to put their strongest reason either first or last, where it will stand out the most. In the example below from "What Was the Purpose of the Inca's Knotted Strings?" the author introduces a paragraph with a strong fact about identical patterns.

> Researchers found an identical three-knot pattern in the strings of seven different quipus. They think the order of the knots is code for the name of an Incan city. They hope to reconstruct the quipu code based on this and other repeating patterns of knots.

Now use the above paragraph as a model to write about your opinion. In the first sentence, try to use a strong reason why you hold the opinion.

_____

_____

_____

_____

Write a Draft Use your web to help you write your draft in your writer's notebook. Don't forget to carefully order your facts and details.

Word Wise

An author's voice can have a formal or informal tone. When authors write persuasive articles, they may use words such as *believe* instead of *think* and *assert* instead of *say*. Words such as *assert* are a type of academic language that can give your writing a formal tone.

Revise

Precise Language Writing should be coherent, or easy to follow. To improve sentence structure and word choice, use precise language. Do not repeat words and phrases in the same sentence. Also, avoid using words with similar meanings in the same sentence. Read the passage below. Then revise it by deleting unnecessary ideas.

> The quipu, an invention of the Incas, was perhaps used by the Incas in the Inca Empire to keep track of data. The quipu has strings and knots, and the strings and knots were likely a representation of data used by the Incas. Some archaeologists believe the Incas used the quipu to perhaps keep track of crops grown in the Inca Empire.

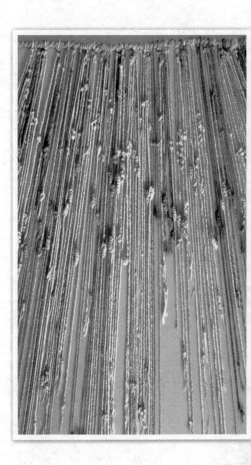

 Revision Revise your draft, and check that you use as much precise language as possible to make your writing coherent.

Peer Conferences

Review a Draft Listen carefully as a partner reads his or her work aloud. Take notes about what you liked and what was difficult to follow. Begin by telling what you liked about the draft. Ask questions that will help the writer think more about the writing. Make suggestions that you think will make the writing stronger. Use these sentence starters.

I enjoyed this part of your draft because . . .

You might want to rethink the order of the facts in . . .

I have a question about . . .

This part is unclear to me. Can you explain why . . . ?

Partner Feedback After your partner gives you feedback on your draft, write one of the suggestions that you will use in your revision. Refer to the rubric on page 85 as you give feedback.

Based on my partner's feedback, I will _____

_____

_____

After you finish giving each other feedback, reflect on the peer conference. What was helpful? What might you do differently next time?

Revision As you revise your draft, use the Revising Checklist to help you figure out what text you may need to move, elaborate on, or delete. Remember to use the rubric on page 85 to help you with your revision.

Revising Checklist

- [ ] Does my writing fit my purpose and audience?
- [ ] Have I clearly stated my claim on the topic?
- [ ] What information can I add to show logical order?
- [ ] Have I used precise language?

Edit and Proofread

When you **edit** and **proofread** your writing, you look for and correct mistakes in spelling, punctuation, capitalization, and grammar. Reading through a revised draft multiple times can help you make sure you're catching any errors. Use the checklist below to edit your article.

✓ Editing Checklist

- ☐ Do all sentences begin with a capital letter and end with a punctuation mark?
- ☐ Are there any run-on sentences or sentence fragments?
- ☐ Are all verbs used correctly?
- ☐ Are proper nouns capitalized?
- ☐ Are quotation marks used correctly?
- ☐ Are all words spelled correctly?

List two mistakes you found as you proofread your persuasive article.

1 _____

_____

2 _____

_____

Grammar Connections

When you proofread your article, make sure that all verbs, including irregular ones, are used correctly. Irregular verbs do not simply add -d or -ed in the past form. For example, the past tense of *think* is *thought*.

Publish, Present, and Evaluate

Publishing When you **publish** your writing, you create a clean, neat final copy that is free of mistakes. Adding visuals can make your writing more interesting. Consider including illustrations, photos, or maps to help make your article more interesting.

Presentation When you are ready to **present** your work, rehearse your presentation. Use the Presenting Checklist to help you.

Evaluate After you publish your writing, use the rubric below to **evaluate** your writing.

What did you do successfully? _____

What needs more work? _____

_____

_____

✔ Presenting Checklist

☐ Stand up straight.

☐ Make eye contact with the audience.

☐ Speak clearly, slowly, and loud enough to be heard.

☐ Display visuals so that everyone can see them.

☐ Answer questions thoughtfully.

4	3	2	1
• clearly states the topic and a point of view • presents several facts and details in a logical order to support a position • precise language is used throughout the article	• states a topic but may not include a clear point of view • presents some facts and details, but they may not be in a logical order • some precise language is used	• states a topic but not a point of view • presents few facts and details, not in a logical order • very little precise language is used	• does not focus on a particular topic or point of view • does not present relevant or convincing facts and details • little or no precise language is used

SHOW WHAT YOU LEARNED

Spiral Review

You have learned new skills and strategies in Unit 3 that will help you read more critically. Now it is time to practice what you have learned.

- **Main Idea and Key Details**
- **Diagrams**
- **Problem and Solution**
- **Context Clues**
- **Dialogue**
- **Theme**
- **Make Inferences**

Connect to Content

- **Create a Sidebar**
- **Parts of a Dolphin**

Read the selection and choose the best answer to each question.

Teamwork and DESTINY

1   The winds blew strongly on December 17, 1903, in the small town of Kitty Hawk, North Carolina. After several years of hard work, Orville and Wilbur Wright's perseverance finally paid off. On that fateful day, they launched a successful flight of an aircraft using a gasoline-powered engine. That flight lasted only 12 seconds, but the accomplishment guaranteed the Wright Brothers a permanent place in the history books. Throughout their lives, their teamwork led to great things.

2   Wilbur Wright was born on April 16, 1867. Four years later, his brother, Orville, was born on August 19, 1871. From an early age, both boys showed strong mechanical abilities. Their parents, Milton and Susan Wright, encouraged this learning. In 1878, their father gave them a rubber band-powered helicopter. Fascinated by it, they built their own copies. This set the stage for their lifelong desire to build flying machines.

3   Early in their adulthood, the Wright brothers worked in the printing business. While they had had some success doing this work, it did not satisfy their need to build things. In the early 1890s, the bicycle business was booming in the United States. Orville and Wilbur finally found a suitable job to satisfy their needs. They opened their own bicycle sales and repair shop. Shortly thereafter, they began to manufacture their own bicycles. The wheels of history continued to turn on the road to the Wright Brothers' destiny.

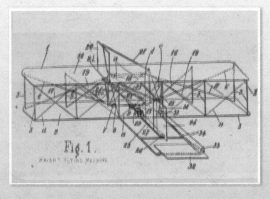

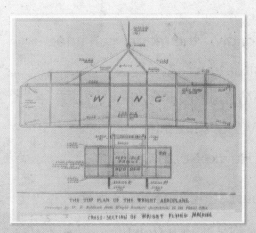

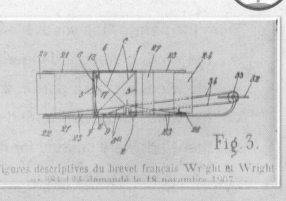

Patent plans for the Wright Brothers' airplane.

4   The Wright Cycle Company was quite profitable, but the Wright Brothers cared little about money. They decided to turn their attention to flying machines. The brothers looked at the work of other flying pioneers to inspire them. They used the work of their predecessors to guide them with their own designs. In 1900, they built their first glider. This biplane managed to fly 300 feet but had many problems. In 1901, Orville and Wilbur decided to construct a larger glider. This glider was not very successful. It did not have enough lift, which is the force that holds a machine in the air. It was also difficult to control.

5   The brothers went back to the drawing board. They designed 200 model wings and tested them in a wind tunnel. This experiment proved successful. In 1902, their third glider became a fully controllable aircraft. The next stage in their journey would prove to be the most challenging—creating an engine-powered aircraft. The Wright Brothers enlisted the help of their mechanic, Charlie Taylor. With his help, they designed a lightweight gasoline engine powerful enough to propel their aircraft. It was this design that led to their first successful flight in 1903. For the next two years, the Wright Brothers made additional flights, making adjustments to perfect their airplane as needed. By 1905, they had created a practical airplane. It was able to remain in the air until its fuel ran out.

6   The Wright Brothers demonstrated that teamwork and determination can lead to endless possibilities. What started as a curiosity about simple machines blossomed into one of the greatest inventions of the 20th century. The world was forever changed on December 17, 1903.

Library of Congress Prints and Photographs Division LC-USZ62-127779]

SHOW WHAT YOU LEARNED

1 From the phrase "the winds blew strongly," the reader can infer —

   A the winds created a dangerous situation

   B the winds played a part in the Wright Brothers' flight

   C the winds almost prevented the Wright Brothers' flight

   D the winds were unusual for Kitty Hawk, North Carolina

2 Which sentence from paragraph 2 best states the main idea?

   F *From an early age, both boys showed strong mechanical abilities.*

   G *Their parents, Milton and Susan Wright, encouraged this learning.*

   H *In 1878, their father gave them a rubber band-powered helicopter.*

   J *Fascinated by it, they built their own copies.*

3 The author includes diagrams to help the reader understand —

   A how an airplane is different from a helicopter

   B the parts of the Wright Brothers' toy helicopter

   C how hard the Wright Brothers worked

   D the parts of the Wright Brothers' airplane

4 In paragraphs 4 and 5, the author shows how the Wright Brothers —

   F took steps to solve the problems with their early aircrafts

   G decided to build planes

   H had problems with the bicycle company

   J built a perfect airplane

Quick Tip

For multiple choice questions, when two answers seem correct, contrast them to identify differences. Then, go back to the question to see if you can choose the best answer.

Read the selection and choose the best answer to each question.

The Promise of a
PAPER LANTERN

1   Dao awoke before the rest of the family, dressed, and made a steaming cup of hot tea. She went outside into the cool morning and sat on the porch, looking out over her family's rice farm. She enjoyed these mornings alone in the quiet misty highlands of Northern Thailand. Normally, she would use this time to think about the day ahead—her studies and her chores. Today was different. She found herself feeling anxious as her thoughts drifted to a talk she had overheard between her parents the previous evening.

2   "The rice paddy is drier than it should be. If we don't get rain soon, we may lose the crop," Dao's father confided with worry.

3   "Surely, rain is coming. I can't remember the last time we've gone so many days without it," Dao's mother reassured him.

4   November was usually such a happy time for the family as they anticipated two grand yearly events: the rice harvest and the <u>festival</u> of Yi Peng. This year, with the rice crop in danger, Dao found it hard to think about the celebration.

5   "Dao, are you still going to help me make a paper lantern today? You promised. The festival is tomorrow," Dao's little brother Gamon interrupted her morning thoughts.

6   Dao tried to smile away her earlier worry. "Of course, Gamon, help me find the rice paper, bamboo, and candles." Dao grabbed the little boy's hand in hers as they hurried into the house.

7   The next evening, Dao, Gamon, and their parents gathered with the other villagers in the center of town. Worry over the lack of rain and the future of the rice crop had been set aside for the night. It was time to celebrate. Everyone held a lantern constructed of thin rice paper stretched over a bamboo frame that held a small candle just like the ones Dao and Gamon had made the day before. After the parade and the fireworks, the people would light the candles in their lanterns. The hot air trapped inside the lanterns would cause them to float up into the sky.

8   Dao's father lit the candle in Gamon's lantern and then the candle in Dao's. As Dao lifted her lantern for release, she thought about a reason to celebrate: She was among friends and family. She smiled to herself as her lantern drifted skyward to join the others. Rain was coming, of course. The night sky filled with brightly lit lanterns seemed like a promise that rain would come.

1. By the end of the story, the reader can infer that Dao —

   A   is secretly worried the drought will continue

   B   thinks positively about the possibility of rain

   C   will find a solution to the lack of rain

   D   will tell Gamon that the family is in trouble

2. The word <u>festival</u> in paragraph 4 means —

   F   a time to plant crops

   G   a time in November

   H   a large meal

   J   a happy gathering

3. The dialogue in paragraph 6 shows —

   A   the amount of time it takes to make a paper lantern

   B   the fact that Dao and Gamon have a close relationship

   C   the uncomfortable situation in Dao's home

   D   the problem that Dao and her family face

4. What is the main theme in the story?

   F   Tradition can help people find hope in difficult times.

   G   Kindness between siblings is good for families.

   H   Children should not listen in on talks between parents.

   J   Family members should trust each other when things are tough.

Quick Tip

For multiple-choice questions, read each answer carefully. Eliminate the ones you know are wrong. If you can't decide between two answers, reread the selection. Look for evidence that can help you answer the question.

ANALYZE HYPERBOLE

COLLABORATE

Writers often use **hyperbole** to emphasize a point. Hyperbole is an exaggeration that is not meant to be taken literally. In the **Literature Anthology** on page 191 of the realistic fiction text *They Don't Mean It!* the narrator uses hyperbole when she says that at Thanksgiving dinner, she stuffed herself until she was bursting. The narrator is not actually bursting. She just means that she overate. Work with a partner to answer the following question.

What is the narrator trying to emphasize with each of these examples?

- She says that she worked harder than anybody at doing the right thing.

_____

- She says that chocolate eggs were everywhere.

_____

MAIN IDEA AND KEY DETAILS

To find the main idea of a text, identify key details and decide what they have in common. Reread ". . . To Beat" on page 197 of the **Literature Anthology**. Use key details to find the main idea of this section. Write it here.

_____

Now write a brief composition about how cultures from other countries have contributed to American culture. A brief composition can be a paragraph or a few paragraphs. It includes a central idea and details that support the idea.

IDENTIFY THE PURPOSE OF INSETS

COLLABORATE

An **inset** is a small illustration inserted within the border of a larger one. Its purpose is to show more detail.

- Review the insets on pages 2 and 3 of the story "A Reluctant Traveler."

- With a partner, identify the purpose of each inset.

Inset	Purpose
passport	
photograph	
map	

Now, imagine that Paul will travel to Texas next. What inset would you add to a map of Texas and why?

Inset	Purpose

The Texas State Capitol in Austin, Texas

Lisandro Luis Trarbach/Shutterstock.com

CREATE A SIDEBAR

A **sidebar** is short, boxed content that appears alongside a main text. Its purpose is to add more information about the topic. A sidebar may also explain an idea that is related to the main text.

- In the **Literature Anthology,** review the sidebar on page 197 of "Where Did That Come From?" Does this sidebar add information or explain an idea related to the main text?

_____

- With a partner, think of possible sidebars that could be added to the other expository texts in this unit.

Text	Possible Sidebar
"Helping Hands," page 214	
"Dig this Technology!" page 222	

Research music, food, or clothing in the United States that has come from other places. Create a second sidebar for "Where Did That Come From?" Write some of your ideas below.

_____

_____

PARTS OF A DOLPHIN

Like all living organisms, a dolphin has body parts that help it to survive. When a body part gets damaged, it must heal or be replaced. As a result, a dolphin may develop a different way of swimming as Winter did in the **Literature Anthology** expository text *Winter's Tail.*

- Research parts of a dolphin and their different uses. List them in the chart.
- Then, label some of a dolphin's body parts on the diagram.

Swimming & Speed	Breathing	Hunting & Eating	Avoiding Predators

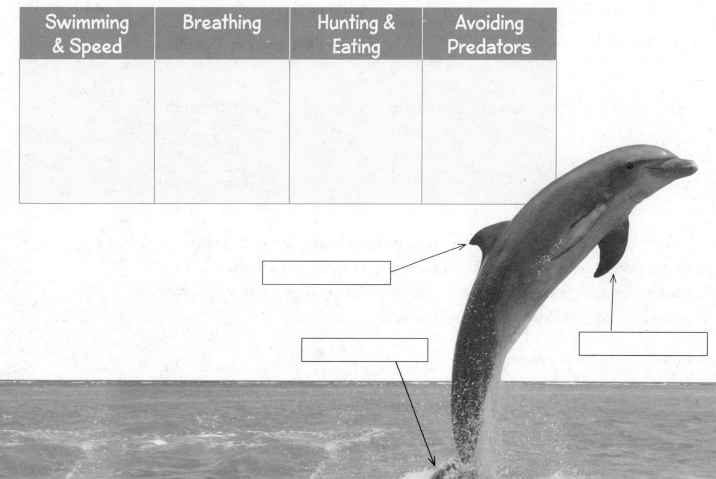

Martin Ruegner/Radius Images/Getty Images

WHAT DID YOU LEARN?

Use the rubric to evaluate yourself on the skills you learned in this unit.
Write your scores in the boxes below.

4	3	2	1
I can successfully identify all examples of this skill.	I can identify most examples of this skill.	I can identify a few examples of this skill.	I need to work on this skill more.

☐ Context Clues   ☐ Latin Roots   ☐ Author's Point of View

☐ Theme   ☐ Main Idea and Key Details

Something that I need to work more on is _____ because

_____

_____

_____

Text to Self Think back over the texts that you have read in this unit.
Choose one text and write a short paragraph explaining a personal
connection that you have made to the text. Making a personal connection
will deepen your understanding of the text.

I made a personal connection to _____ because _____

_____

_____

SOCIAL STUDIES

Present Your Work

COLLABORATE

Discuss how you will share your presentation about ancestors of a Native American civilization. Then discuss the sentence starters below and write your answers.

Use the Listening Checklist as your classmates give their presentations.

Tech Tip

Make sure the equipment is set up and working properly in order to play any audio or visual features in your presentation.

Listening Checklist

- ☐ Listen actively by taking notes on the presenter's ideas.
- ☐ Pay attention to nonverbal cues, such as facial expressions.
- ☐ Ask relevant questions.
- ☐ Provide feedback and make pertinent comments.

In my research about ancestors of a Native American civilization, I learned

_____

_____

_____

If I visited a site, I would like to see _____

_____

_____

Hero Images/Getty Images

MR. PRESIDENT HOW LONG MUST WOMEN WAIT FOR LIBERTY

COLLABORATE

Society is made up of the citizens, or people, in a community or country. Throughout history, outspoken citizens have challenged laws they believed to be unfair. For example, at one time, women in the United States could not vote in elections. They wanted to change this.

Look at the photo. What actions are the women taking? Turn to your partner and discuss what you think the women want to change. Write what people in society do to make positive changes in the web.

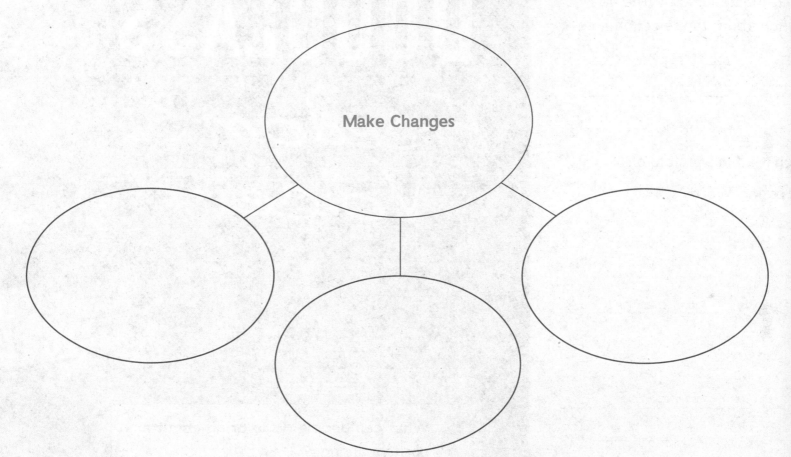

Make Changes

Go online to **my.mheducation.com** and read the "Liberty and Justice for All" Blast. Think about the freedoms and rights that we have today in the United States. What would you do if you did not have these rights? Then blast back your response.

TAKE NOTES

Asking questions about a text and then looking for answers helps you gain information. Before you read, look at the headings. Write a question about the selection here.

_____

_____

_____

As you read, make note of:

Interesting Words _____

_____

_____

Key Details _____

_____

_____

_____

_____

FREDERICK DOUGLASS

Freedom's Voice

Essential Question

What can people do to bring about a positive change?

Read about what Frederick Douglass did to bring about positive change for African Americans.

Growing Up with Slavery

When Frederick Douglass was growing up in Maryland, he never could have imagined that he would become a great civil rights leader. Born Frederick Bailey, he was enslaved, or living in slavery, until the age of twenty. Frederick's life was difficult. He never knew his father and was separated from his mother at a young age. If he dared to **defy** his "master" in any way, he was punished. One of the few bright spots of his youth was being taught to read by the wife of a slave holder. Perhaps it was his love of words, along with his courage, that inspired Frederick to reach for the kind of life he was **entitled** to have.

▼ This etching depicts a slave auction, a common event of the time.

A Life-Changing Speech

In 1838 Frederick **sought** his freedom by escaping to the North. In New York City, he married Anna Murray. Then he and Anna moved to New Bedford, Massachusetts.

In New Bedford, Frederick changed his last name to Douglass to protect himself against slave catchers. That was just the first of many changes. He also discovered a group of people—abolitionists—who shared his hope of ending slavery. He had read about the abolition movement in William Lloyd Garrison's newspaper, *The Liberator*. Frederick devoured every issue because the ideas inspired him so much. Soon he began speaking against slavery at the church meetings he attended.

FIND TEXT EVIDENCE

Read

Paragraph 1

Author's Point of View

Underline two details that tell about slavery. What is the author's point of view?

_____

_____

Paragraphs 2–3

Summarize

Summarize Douglass's life in the North.

_____

_____

_____

_____

_____

Reread

Author's Craft

How does the author help you understand how interested Douglass was in the abolition movement?

FIND TEXT EVIDENCE 🔍

Read

Paragraphs 1–3

Summarize

Summarize Douglass's feelings before, during, and after speaking at the Anti-Slavery Society.

_____

_____

_____

_____

_____

Paragraph 4

Author's Point of View

Circle the words that show how the author <u>feels</u> about Douglass as a <u>speaker</u>.

Reread

Author's Craft

How does the author help you understand how the abolitionists responded to Douglass?

New Opportunities

In 1841, The Massachusetts Anti-Slavery Society held a meeting in Nantucket. Frederick was eager to hear the abolitionist speakers and traveled to the meeting with **anticipation.** However, when he arrived, something totally unexpected happened. An abolitionist who had heard Frederick speak at a church meeting asked him to speak to this large gathering!

Frederick went to the front of the meeting hall, trembling with fright. At first, he spoke quietly and hesitantly. He felt anxious standing in front of so many people—especially white people! However, once he got started, his fear evaporated. He spoke from his heart, describing the horrors of slavery. Frederick was a stirring speaker, articulate and **outspoken.** At the end of his speech, the audience's reaction was spontaneous—suddenly everyone stood up and cheered! Among those cheering was none other than William Lloyd Garrison.

After the meeting, Garrison congratulated Frederick and offered him a job as a speaker for the Society. Frederick agreed and was hired as a full-time lecturer. He felt he had found a purpose for his life.

Frederick traveled through New England and the Midwest, giving passionate speeches that captivated audiences. It was impossible to listen to his (powerful) words and remain **neutral.** Frederick had a commanding presence and spoke with (eloquence) and dignity. He was making a name for himself.

North Wind Picture Archives/Alamy Stock Photo

Making His Mark

In addition to giving speeches, Frederick had time **reserved** for his writing. In 1845 he wrote an autobiography, *Narrative of the Life of Frederick Douglass, an American Slave*. The book became a huge success, making him even more famous.

In his autobiography, Frederick revealed that he was a fugitive. For his safety, friends suggested that he go on a speaking tour in Great Britain. Frederick was very popular there, and people lined up to hear him speak.

▲ The North Star was the newspaper published by Frederick Douglass and his wife.

▲ Douglass's autobiography helped advance abolition.

In 1847 Frederick returned to the United States. By now, he had a family and missed them terribly. Upon his return, they moved to Rochester, New York, where Frederick started his own abolitionist newspaper. *The North Star* was an unusual newspaper. It published articles not only about the antislavery cause, but also about the **unequal** status of women. Frederick also worked tirelessly to end segregation in Rochester's schools.

Summarize

Use your notes and the illustrations, photos, and captions to orally summarize what you learned about Frederick Douglass.

FIND TEXT EVIDENCE 🔍

Read

Paragraph 1

Suffixes

The suffix *-ive* means "having the nature of." How does the suffix help you determine the meaning of *narrative*? Write your answer here.

_____

_____

_____

Paragraphs 2–3

Photographs and Captions

What do the photographs show?

Douglass's autobiography helped advance abolition.

Underline the new information about Douglass in the captions.

Reread

Author's Craft

Why do you think the author used the subhead "Making His Mark" for this section of the text?

(t) Todd Bigelow/Aurora Photos; (b) Everett Collection Inc./Alamy Stock Photo

Vocabulary

Use the example sentences to talk with a partner about each word. Then answer the questions.

anticipation

The goalie waited with **anticipation** as the ball came toward her.

What is something that you have waited for with anticipation?

_____

_____

defy

If you **defy** a driving rule, you may get a ticket.

Why might someone defy a rule or law?

_____

_____

entitled

The library card **entitled** Matt to check out a book.

What phrase has the same meaning as entitled?

_____

_____

neutral

An umpire must stay **neutral** when making a call on a play.

Why must an umpire or referee stay neutral during a game?

_____

_____

outspoken

Jake is **outspoken** about protecting the environment.

What word has the opposite meaning of outspoken?

_____

_____

Build Your Word List Pick a word you found interesting in the selection you read. Look up synonyms and antonyms of the word in a thesaurus and write them in your writer's notebook.

reserved

Some parking spaces are **reserved** for people with babies.

What other things can be reserved?

_____

_____

_____

sought

Josie **sought** the missing puzzle piece.

What was something you sought and were able to find?

_____

_____

_____

unequal

The number of players on the tug-of-war teams was **unequal**.

If two teams are unequal, what might the game be like?

_____

_____

_____

Prefixes and Suffixes

Prefixes are added to the beginnings of words and change their meanings. The prefix *un-* means "not." The prefix *en-* means "to make." **Suffixes** are added to the ends of words and change their meanings. The suffix *–ive* means "having the nature of." The suffixes *–er* and *–or* mean "a person who."

🔍 FIND TEXT EVIDENCE

When I read the word enslaved, *I can use the prefix* en- *to figure out the meaning of the word. Since* en- *means "to make,"* enslaved *must mean "made a slave."*

Born Frederick Bailey, he was enslaved, or living in slavery, until the age of twenty.

Your Turn Use the prefix or suffix to figure out the meanings of the following words in "Frederick Douglass: Freedom's Voice."

liberator, *page 101* _____

unexpected, *page 102* _____

Summarize

When you summarize, you sort the most important ideas and key details and retell them in your own words. This helps you to monitor comprehension and remember what you have learned. Reread, use background knowledge, and ask questions to make adjustments as you read.

Quick Tip

When you summarize a long text, make a list of all the important details. Then, read through the list and add only the ones that are the most important to your summary.

FIND TEXT EVIDENCE

To make sure you understand the most important details of "Growing Up with Slavery" on page 101, you can summarize the most important points.

Page 101

Born Frederick Bailey, he was enslaved, or living in slavery, until the age of twenty. Frederick's life was difficult. He never knew his father and was separated from his mother at a young age. If he dared to **defy** his "master" in any way, he was punished. One of the few bright spots of his youth was being taught to read by the wife of a slave holder. Perhaps it was his love of words, along with his courage, that inspired Frederick to reach for the kind of life he was **entitled** to have.

Frederick Douglass spent the first twenty years of his life in slavery. He was sent away from his mother at an early age, was punished by his "master," and was taught to read by a slave holder's wife. Learning to read inspired him.

Your Turn Use the most important ideas and key details to summarize the rest of the biography. Use the Summarize strategy as you read other texts.

_____

_____

_____

_____

Photographs and Captions

The selection "Frederick Douglass: Freedom's Voice" is a biography.
A biography tells facts about the life of a real person. It describes the
person's talents and achievements. A biography is often written in logical
order and often includes **photographs** and **captions**.

🔍 FIND TEXT EVIDENCE

*I can tell that "Frederick Douglass: Freedom's Voice" is a biography.
Frederick Douglass was a real person, and the photographs show real
people and events. The selection tells about his talents and achievements,
and the events are told in logical order.*

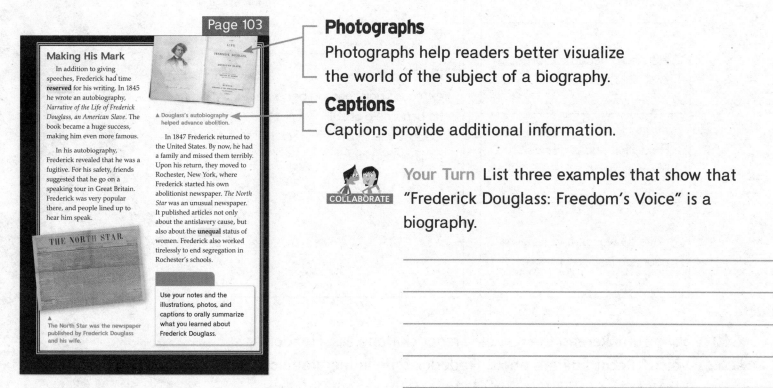

Page 103

Making His Mark

In addition to giving
speeches, Frederick had time
reserved for his writing. In 1845
he wrote an autobiography,
*Narrative of the Life of Frederick
Douglass, an American Slave*. The
book became a huge success,
making him even more famous.

In his autobiography,
Frederick revealed that he was a
fugitive. For his safety, friends
suggested that he go on a
speaking tour in Great Britain.
Frederick was very popular
there, and people lined up to
hear him speak.

▲ Douglass's autobiography
helped advance abolition.

In 1847 Frederick returned to
the United States. By now, he had
a family and missed them terribly.
Upon his return, they moved to
Rochester, New York, where
Frederick started his own
abolitionist newspaper. *The North
Star* was an unusual newspaper.
It published articles not only
about the antislavery cause, but
also about the **unequal** status of
women. Frederick also worked
tirelessly to end segregation in
Rochester's schools.

THE NORTH STAR.

▲
The North Star was the newspaper
published by Frederick Douglass
and his wife.

Use your notes and the
illustrations, photos, and
captions to orally summarize
what you learned about
Frederick Douglass.

Photographs
Photographs help readers better visualize
the world of the subject of a biography.

Captions
Captions provide additional information.

Your Turn List three examples that show that
"Frederick Douglass: Freedom's Voice" is a
biography.

COLLABORATE

_____

_____

_____

_____

_____

Author's Point of View

An **author's point of view** is the author's attitude toward the person or subject he or she is writing about. You can determine an author's point of view by looking at the details, descriptions, and the reasons and evidence for points the author makes.

🔍 **FIND TEXT EVIDENCE**

On page 101, the words tell that the author thinks highly of Frederick Douglass. The author says that Douglass would become a great civil rights leader.

Details	Author's Point of View
He would become a great civil rights leader.	Frederick was an extraordinary person because he became a great civil rights leader in spite of his difficult beginning in life.
Frederick had a difficult life in slavery.	
Love of words and his own courage inspired him.	

Your Turn Reread the rest of "Frederick Douglass: Freedom's Voice." Record details about Frederick's life in the graphic organizer on page 109. Then tell the author's point of view.

North Wind Picture Archives/Alamy Stock Photo

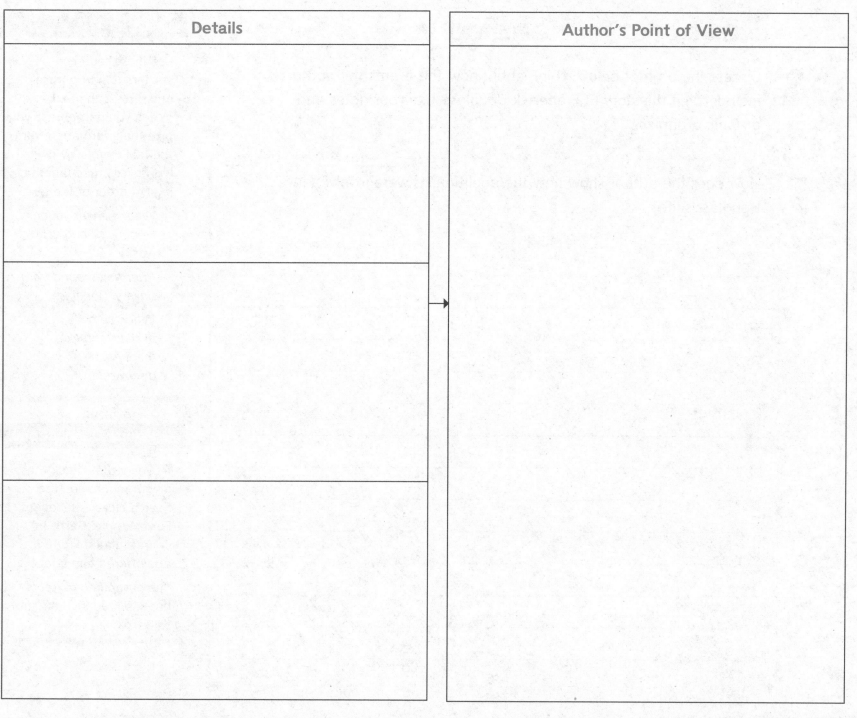

Details	Author's Point of View

Respond to Reading

Discuss the prompt below. Think about how the events the author included tell the story of Frederick Douglass. Use your notes and graphic organizer.

How does the author show how the abolitionists were involved in Douglass's life?

_____

_____

_____

_____

_____

_____

_____

_____

_____

_____

_____

_____

_____

Quick Tip

Use these sentence starters to paraphrase and discuss the text. When you paraphrase you give the information from the text in your own words. You maintain the logical order of the text.

- *When he was young, Frederick Douglass was . . .*
- *After he escaped from slavery, Douglass . . .*
- *When he gave a speech at the Nantucket meeting, he discovered . . .*

Grammar Connections

As you write, check that any pronouns you use have a clear antecedent. For example: Garrison congratulated Frederick and offered **him** a job.

The pronoun *him* refers back to Frederick and not to Garrison.

Create a Bibliography

A **bibliography** is a list of books, magazines, articles, and websites used for research on a topic. Here are tips for creating entries:

- List a book by author's last name, first name, book title, city of publication, publisher, and copyright date.

- List an article by author's last name, first name, article title, newspaper or magazine title, and date of the issue.

- List an online article by the author's last name, first name, article title, website name, publication date, and date accessed.

Why is it important to list your sources? Write your answer.

_____

_____

Design a Plaque With a partner, research a person who played an important part in the Civil Rights Movement. Choose someone you want to learn about. A teacher or other adult can help you develop and follow a research plan. Then design a plaque in honor of the person. A plaque is a flat piece of metal or wood that has writing on it. It might be mounted on a building or surface.

For your design, include a brief history of the person. Add a quote from the person or a quote about the person. Discuss any art you may want to include. Remember to have an adult help you. Develop a bibliography of all sources you use. After you complete your plaque's design, you will present your work to your class.

Dr. Martin Luther King, Jr. (1929–1968) was a civil rights leader whose actions led to positive changes.

Consolidated News Pictures/Hulton Archive/Getty Images

Rosa

? **How does the author help you visualize what Rosa was like?**

Literature Anthology: pages 262–277

COLLABORATE

Talk About It Reread the last paragraph on **Literature Anthology** page 265. Discuss with your partner what Rosa does when she sits on the bus.

Cite Text Evidence What words and phrases help create a mental image of what Rosa was like? Write text evidence in the chart.

Evaluate Information

Illustrations can help you to understand the text. How does the illustration help you to visualize Rosa and understand what kind of person she was?

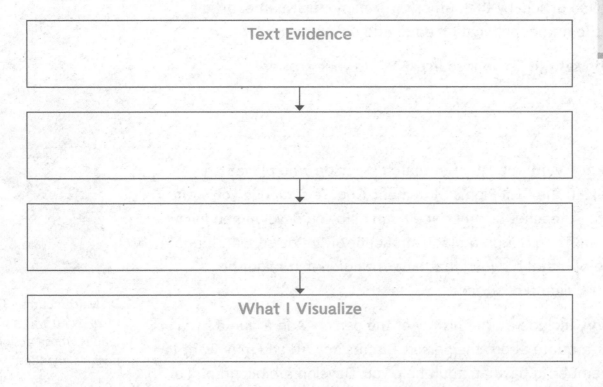

Text Evidence

↓

↓

↓

What I Visualize

Write The author helps me understand what Rosa was like by _____

_____

How do you know what Rosa thinks and how she feels as she sits on the bus waiting for the police?

Talk About It Reread **Literature Anthology** page 268. Turn to a partner and talk about what Rosa thinks about on the bus.

Cite Text Evidence What words and phrases help you know what Rosa is thinking and feeling? Write text evidence in the chart.

What Rosa Thinks	What It Shows

Write I know what Rosa is thinking and feeling on the bus because

the author _____

_____

_____

Quick Tip

When you read, picture in your mind what the author is describing. This helps you understand what Rosa is thinking and feeling.

Make Inferences

What does the author mean when she writes that all the people through all those many years joined Rosa? How does this line help you understand Rosa's actions?

? **Why does the author use Martin Luther King, Jr.'s quote?**

COLLABORATE

Talk About It Reread the last paragraph on **Literature Anthology** page 272. Turn to a partner and talk about what Martin Luther King, Jr. said.

Cite Text Evidence What does Martin Luther King, Jr.'s quote mean? Cite text evidence and tell why the author includes it in the selection.

Quick Tip

Figurative language does not mean exactly what it says. A simile compares two things using *like* or *as*. A metaphor compares two things without using *like* or *as*. As you read, look for *like* or *as* and think about what is being compared.

Text Evidence		What It Means
	→	
	→	
	→	

Write The author uses Martin Luther King, Jr.'s quote to help me understand _____

_____

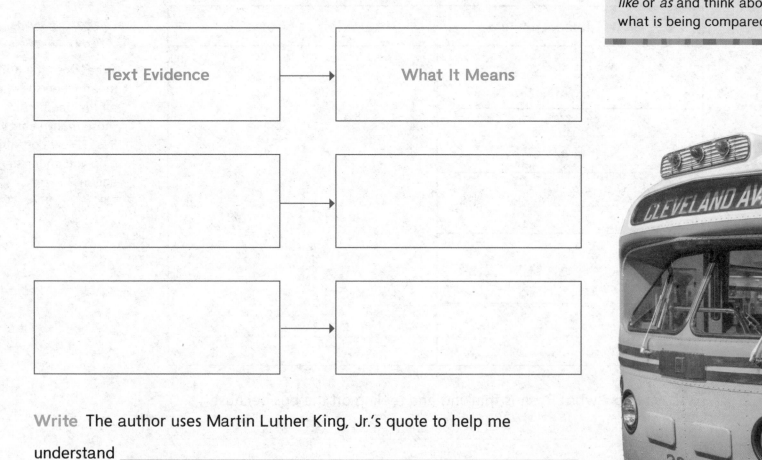

Ian Dagnall Commercial Collection/Alamy Stock Photo

Respond to Reading

COLLABORATE

Discuss the prompt below. Apply your own knowledge of figurative language such as similes and metaphors to inform your answer. Use your notes and graphic organizer.

How does Nikki Giovanni use figurative language to help you understand the theme, or message, of this selection?

Our Voices, Our Votes

Literature Anthology:
pages 280-283

Rights for African Americans

1 During the early 1800s, many women's groups joined with abolitionists to demand equal rights. Abolitionists were people who wanted to end slavery. They believed that freedom was a natural right. Women marched with them in protest. Some of them helped enslaved people escape to places where they could be free. Over 300 people gathered at a convention in Seneca Falls, New York in 1848. They discussed how women's rights were linked to other social and civil rights movements. Some speakers urged that suffrage, or voting rights, be a top priority for African Americans and women.

2 After the Civil War, the United States government added the Thirteenth Amendment, outlawing slavery. Three years later, the Fourteenth Amendment granted former slaves rights as citizens. Finally, in 1870, the Fifteenth Amendment gave male citizens of all races the right to vote. Though many women supported these causes, women still could not vote. Their fight was far from over.

Reread paragraph 1. **Circle** the sentence in the first paragraph that helps you understand who abolitionists were.

Then **underline** the sentence that explains how the abolitionists and women who wanted suffrage were alike.

Reread paragraph 2. Talk with a partner about how the author organizes information. **Write** numbers in the margin to indicate the order in which the laws changed.

Women's Suffrage

3 Women continued to fight for suffrage on the national, state, and local levels. Some were outraged enough to defy voting laws and attempt to cast ballots in elections. These acts of civil disobedience resulted in fines. In some cases, the women ended up in jail.

4 Women's suffrage remained unpopular with many men. Even so, the idea took hold in some areas. In 1869, Wyoming became the first state to allow women to vote in its elections. Over the next twenty years, four more states would grant women this right.

5 Women began to join forces, borrowing ideas from women's groups in other countries. Some hired lobbyists, or people who tried to convince politicians to vote a certain way. Others held huge rallies to raise awareness. Petitions bearing thousands of signatures demanded that the country's laws be amended.

6 President Woodrow Wilson finally agreed that a true democracy should not deny women the right to vote. With his support, Congress drafted the Nineteenth Amendment to the Constitution. In 1920, it was approved.

How do you know that suffrage was an important issue for women? **Underline** the clue in paragraph 1 that helps you understand how big a struggle it was.

Reread paragraph 5. **Circle** the ways women took action. Write them here:

1. _____

2. _____

3. _____

4. _____

COLLABORATE

Talk with a partner about how President Woodrow Wilson influenced how women achieved the right to vote. **Draw a box** around the text evidence to support your discussion.

? **Why is "Our Voices, Our Votes" a good title for this selection?**

COLLABORATE

Talk About It Reread paragraph 5 on page 117. Talk with a partner about how women joined forces to make changes in the law.

Cite Text Evidence What words and phrases help you understand how women worked together to change the voting laws? Write text evidence.

✂ Evaluate Information

A voice is made up of sounds, but a voice is also an opinion or choice. Why do you think the author uses the word *Voices* in the title?

Detail

↓

Detail

↓

Detail

↓

What It Means

Write "Our Voices, Our Votes" is a good title for this selection because

_____

_____

Abigail Adams supported women's right to vote.

Bettmann/Getty Images

Text Structure

As authors plan their writing, they think about how to best structure their text so that it contributes to their purpose. For example, authors who write informational text about historical events may structure text in a logical order, such as sequence of events.

FIND TEXT EVIDENCE

On page 116 of "Our Voices, Our Votes," the author structures paragraph 2 in a logical time order to show when Constitutional amendments granted rights to males but not women.

> Finally, in 1870, the Fifteenth Amendment gave male citizens of all races the right to vote.

Your Turn Reread paragraph 4 under "Women's Suffrage" on page 117.

- Why does the author tell about what happened in Wyoming at this point in the text?

  _____

  _____

- How does this contribute to the author's purpose?

  _____

  _____

  _____

Readers to Writers

Before you begin writing, plan a logical order of what you want to say. For historical events, it makes sense to structure your text in time order. Within that structure, think about what is most important to include.

Text Connections

? **How does the photographer show how the men are taking a stand in the same way the authors of *Rosa* and "Our Voices, Our Votes" show how people have taken a stand?**

Talk About It Look at the photograph. Read the caption. Talk with a partner about what the two men are doing. Discuss what you see on the billboard.

Cite Text Evidence **Circle** how the men are taking a stand. **Underline** what they are taking a stand against.

Write The photographer and authors show how people take a stand by _____

_____

_____

_____

_____

_____

"Toward Los Angeles, California" shows two men walking along a highway. The photograph was taken in 1937.

Present Your Work

Discuss how you will present your plans for the plaque honoring a well-known person from the Civil Rights Movement. Use the Presenting Checklist as you practice your presentation. Discuss the sentence starters below and write your answers.

In my research about a person in the Civil Rights Movement, I discovered that _____

_____

_____

_____

I would like to know more about _____

_____

_____

✓ Presenting Checklist

☐ Plan with your partner how you will present your plaque design and read the text you included in the design.

☐ Rehearse your presentation. Explain how you selected the person and designed your plaque.

☐ Speak slowly and clearly.

☐ Make eye contact with your audience.

☐ Have your research ready to help you answer questions.

Expert Model

Literature Anthology:
pages 262-277

Features of a Biography

A biography is an account of someone's life written by someone else. It gives readers information about significant events in the person's life. A biography

- provides information about ways the person has made a difference

- tells what the person did during his or her life, in a logical order

- has a strong conclusion that states why the person is important

Word Wise

On page 267, the author uses words such as *bellowed, muttered, yelled,* and *quietly replied.* Precise verbs make a biography more interesting to read.

Analyze an Expert Model Studying a biography will help you learn how to write a biography of your own. **Reread** page 267 in the **Literature Anthology**. Write your answers to the questions below.

How does the author help you understand Rosa Parks's courageous

actions? _____

_____

_____

How did Rosa Parks make a difference in the world? _____

_____

_____

_____

Plan: Choose Your Topic

Mapping With a partner, talk about people from the past who have made a difference by improving civil rights. These should be people you have not already studied in this unit. On a sheet of paper, create a web to map your ideas.

Writing Prompt Choose one historical figure from your mapping. Write his or her biography.

I will write a biography about _____.

Purpose and Audience Think about your purpose for writing. Are you writing to inform, persuade, or entertain your readers?

My purpose for writing is _____.

Next, think about who will read or hear your biography.

My audience will be _____.

Then, think about the language you will use to write the biography.

I will use _____ language when I write the biography.

Plan In your writer's notebook, make a chart to plan some of the details you will include in your biography. Fill in a detail from the discussion with your partner.

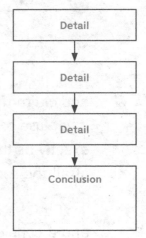

Plan: Focus on a Person

Research Take notes in your writer's notebook about the person you chose by using books, websites, or documentaries. Look for details about the person's life and his or her contributions to civil rights. Choose the events and details you want to include in your biography. As you plan your writing, ask yourself these questions:

- Have I found the most important information about the person's life?

- Does the information include the contributions the person made?

- Do I need to find more reliable sources about this person?

List two important details you might include in your biography.

1 _____

_____

2 _____

_____

Cite Your Sources Avoid plagiarism. Do not copy other people's words and claim them as your own. Paraphrase, or reword, the information. If you use someone else's exact words, put them in quotes exactly as they appear in the source. Provide a bibliography of all the sources you used.

Graphic Organizer Fill in the other details and a conclusion in your Details chart.

1918

Draft

Transitions If the events in your biography are presented in an order that does not make sense, you might confuse your readers. Read the example below from "A Warrior for Women's Rights" and pay close attention to the words that show the sequence of events.

> President Wilson announced that he supported Paul's cause. In 1918, he sent Congress a constitutional amendment that would give women the right to vote. Two years later, the amendment—the 19th—became law.

Now use the excerpt above as a model to write a paragraph for your biography. Use dates as transitions. Also try to use words such as *first, again, before,* and *later* to help link the sequence of events.

_____

_____

_____

_____

Write a Draft Use your Details chart to help you write your draft in your writer's notebook. Write a conclusion that summarizes why the person was an important figure in history.

Revise

Strong Conclusion A biography may end with a conclusion that restates why the person was important. When you conclude your biography, sum up the details and explain how your person contributed to civil rights. Read the paragraph below. Then revise it to improve sentence structure by deleting unnecessary ideas to make a strong, clear conclusion.

Quick Tip

You can improve sentences by deleting unnecessary ideas. For example, write *This happened because* instead of *The reason that this happened is because.*

> Dr. Martin Luther King, Jr. was leader for civil rights in the Civil Rights Movement. He helped plan and organize marches to inspire people to make them stand up for what they believed in and felt was right. These are the reasons why Dr. King is honored and remembered for his actions.

 Revision Revise your draft, check that your conclusion is as strong as possible, and improve sentence structures for clarity.

Peer Conferences

COLLABORATE

Review a Draft Listen carefully as a partner reads his or her work aloud. Take notes about what you liked and what was difficult to follow. Begin by telling what you liked about the draft. Ask questions that will help the writer think more about the writing. Make suggestions that you think will make the writing stronger. Use these sentence starters.

I enjoyed this part of your draft because . . .

The sequence of events is slightly unclear because . . .

I have a question about . . .

This part is unclear to me. Can you explain why . . . ?

Partner Feedback After your partner gives you feedback on your draft, write one of the suggestions that you will use in your revision. Refer to the rubric on page 129 as you give feedback.

Based on my partner's feedback, I will _____

_____

_____

After you finish giving each other feedback, reflect on the peer conference. What was helpful? What might you do differently next time?

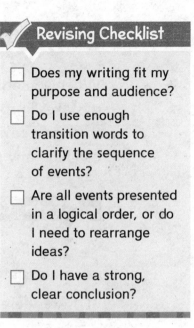

Revision As you revise your draft use the Revising Checklist to help you figure out what text you may need to move, elaborate on, or delete. Remember to use the rubric on page 129 to help you with your revision.

✓ Revising Checklist

☐ Does my writing fit my purpose and audience?

☐ Do I use enough transition words to clarify the sequence of events?

☐ Are all events presented in a logical order, or do I need to rearrange ideas?

☐ Do I have a strong, clear conclusion?

Edit and Proofread

When you **edit** and **proofread** your writing, you look for and correct mistakes in spelling, punctuation, capitalization, and grammar. Reading through a revised draft multiple times can help you make sure you're catching any errors. Use the checklist below to edit your biography.

✓ Editing Checklist

☐ Do all sentences begin with a capital letter and end with a punctuation mark?

☐ Are there any run-on sentences or sentence fragments?

☐ Are all your action verbs used correctly?

☐ Are all pronouns and antecedents in agreement?

☐ Are quotation marks used correctly?

☐ Are all words spelled correctly?

List two mistakes you found as you proofread your biography.

1 _____

2 _____

Publish, Present, and Evaluate

Publishing When you **publish** your writing, you create a clean, neat final copy that is free of mistakes. Adding visuals can make your writing more interesting. Consider including illustrations or photos to make your biography more interesting.

Presentation When you are ready to **present** your work, rehearse your presentation. Use the Presenting Checklist to help you.

Evaluate After you publish your writing, use the rubric below to **evaluate** your writing.

What did you do successfully? _____

What needs more work? _____

_____

Presenting Checklist

☐ Stand up straight.

☐ Look at the audience.

☐ Speak clearly and slowly.

☐ Speak loud enough so that everyone can hear you.

☐ Answer questions thoughtfully using details from your topic.

4	3	2	1
• focuses on a particular person and the person's contributions to civil rights • sequence of events is clear and logical • includes a strong conclusion that restates the main points and explains why the person is important	• focuses on a particular person but not necessarily on the person's contributions to civil rights • sequence of events is mostly logical • includes a conclusion that restates the main points but may not explain why the person is important	• focuses on a particular person but does not focus on the person's contributions to civil rights • sequence of events is somewhat logical • conclusion does not restate main points or explain why the person is important	• does not focus on a particular person • sequence of events is unclear • does not include a strong conclusion that restates the main ideas and explains why the person is important

Talk About It

Essential Question

What can you discover when you give things a second look?

Look at the photo. At first glance, this looks like two buildings next to each other. Now look again. Notice the artist painting the lamp post. How do you interpret that picture?

What do you see as you reconsider this photo? Talk with a partner about what discoveries you made from giving a second look. Write your ideas in the web.

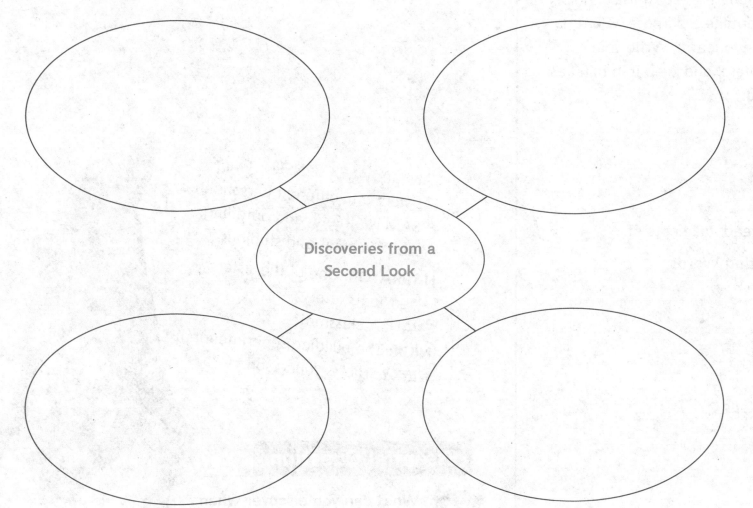

Discoveries from a Second Look

 BLAST BACK! studysync

Go online to **my.mheducation.com** and read the "A Second Glance" Blast. Do you know of any mysteries? What have you discovered when you gave things a second look? Blast back your response.

MIGUEL MEDINA/AFP/Getty Images

TAKE NOTES

Establish a purpose for reading. Preview the title and the character descriptions in the cast list to help you determine a purpose. What do you hope to learn? Write your answer here, and keep it in mind as you read.

_____

_____

_____

As you read, take note of:

Interesting Words _____

_____

_____

_____

Key Details _____

_____

_____

_____

_____

Where's Brownie?

Elizabeth Buttler

CAST

SAM _and_ **ALEX JENSEN:** Twin sisters with different personalities. SAM is athletic and outgoing. ALEX is quiet and studious.

NARRATOR: One of the sisters, ten years later.

EVAN: A classmate.

NICK: The building superintendent.

NICKY: Nick's young son.

Essential Question

What can you discover when you give things a second look?

Read about kids who piece together clues to find a missing pet.

Scene One

Setting: A two-person bedroom in an apartment. SAM sits at a messy desk, creating a poster. EVAN works at a clean desk. Nearby are an empty terrarium and a paper bag that is wet and torn at the bottom.

Narrator: Whoever claimed that "two heads are better than one" never met my twin sister. Half the time, she makes problems worse rather than better. Like when we lost Brownie, our pet chameleon . . .

(ALEX enters. SAM and EVAN quickly cover up their work.)

Alex: How was the science fair? Did everyone like Brownie?

Sam: They did. Mr. Rollins was **astounded** that my exhibit was so good. *(SAM tries to hide the empty terrarium from ALEX.)*

Alex: So where's Brownie? And why is Evan here?

(EVAN and SAM begin texting on hand-held devices.)

Alex: How should I **interpret** this silence? You're making me feel **suspicious**. And, where's Brownie?

Sam: Um, Brownie's missing. But look! Evan and I made these.

*(SAM pulls out a poster she had **concealed** on her desk.)*

Sam: We'll put them up at school tomorrow.

Alex: What makes you think Brownie's back at school?

Sam: Because that's the last place I saw him. In that bag.

Alex: Hey, the bottom of the bag is all wet.

Sam: Maybe it got wet in the lobby. Little Nicky was playing in the fountain with his foldy-paper boat thingies.

Alex: That's origami, to be **precise**. Hey! The bag has a rip.

Sam: Rip? I didn't see a rip. Oh, at the bottom.

Alex: Follow me. I think I know where Brownie is!

Narrator: We raced to the lobby. Brownie had been missing for over an hour, but better late than never!

DRAMA

FIND TEXT EVIDENCE

Read

Page 133
Scenes

Circle the information that tells where Scene One takes place.

Stage Directions

Underline what Sam and Evan do when Alex enters. What does this tell you about Sam and Evan?

_____

_____

Narrator's Last Line
Adages and Proverbs

"Better late than never!" is an adage, a traditional saying. Using context, what does it mean?

_____

_____

_____

Reread

Author's Craft

How does the description of the setting create suspense?

FIND TEXT EVIDENCE 🔍

Read

Page 134

Visualize

Use the setting to create mental images of what is happening in the lobby. What do you visualize?

_____

_____

_____

_____

Nick's Dialogue

Point of View

Circle the text that tells you what Nick thinks about the kids' problem. What does Nick think the kids should do?

bag to apartament

_____

Reread

Author's Craft

How does the author give the readers clues to solving the mystery?

Scene Two

Setting: The lobby of the apartment building. A tall, green, potted plant stands next to a small fountain, where NICKY is playing. ALEX, SAM, and EVAN talk to NICK near a bulletin board.

Nick: So these posters are about your lizard, Brownie. I'm still **perplexed** as to why you think he's down here.

Sam: Because we already checked upstairs.

Alex: Brownie's a chameleon. We think he escaped when Sam set the bag down near the fountain.

Nick: Hey, Nicky! Any brown lizards in the lobby?

Nicky: Nope.

Nick: Maybe you should **reconsider** this and try searching your apartment again.

Evan: Wait a minute. _(checks his device)_ It says here that chameleons climb trees.

Nick: Nicky! Any brown lizards in that tree?

Nicky: Nope.

Evan: It also says that chameleons prefer running water, like that fountain.

Nick: Nicky! Any brown lizards in the fountain?

Nicky: Nope.

Elizabeth Buttler

Nick: What else does that thing say?

Sam: Yeah, **inquisitive** minds want to know.

Alex: *(to SAM)* Don't you want to find Brownie, or are you thinking "out of sight, out of mind"?

Sam: He's just a lizard, Alex. I mean chameleon. It's not exactly "absence makes the heart grow fonder."

Evan: Listen to this! Chameleons change color to match their environments when they're confused or afraid.

Alex: Of course! Nicky, any GREEN lizards over there?

Nicky: *(points into the tree)* There's just that one.

Alex: It's Brownie!

Sam: *(confused)* Brownie has always been brown.

Alex: That's because we put only brown things in his cage, like branches and wood chips.

Evan: Maybe you should buy him a green plant.

Sam: And a little fountain.

Nicky: And boats to go sailing!

Narrator: Well, that's how we found our beloved Brownie, and all was well with the world once more!

Summarize

Use your notes to orally summarize the mystery and how it was solved in "Where's Brownie?" When you summarize, be sure to maintain the meaning of the events and to tell them in logical order.

FIND TEXT EVIDENCE

Read

Page 135

Point of View

Underline the text that shows Alex's feelings about Brownie. **Circle** the text that tells Sam's feelings about Brownie. How are Alex's feelings about Brownie different from Sam's?

Alex does care
Sam doesn't not care

Visualize

Draw a box around the text that tells what Nicky does. What does this help you visualize?

_____

_____

_____

Reread

Author's Craft

Why does the author end with the narrator talking?

Vocabulary

Use the example sentences to talk with a partner about each word. Then answer the questions.

astounded

Jada was **astounded** by her high score in the video game.

What experiences have astounded you?

Birday

concealed

The mask **concealed** the identity of the mysterious superhero.

What other ways have people concealed their identities?

inquisitive

The **inquisitive** girl asked a lot of questions.

How might an inquisitive person find things out?

interpret

My sister is taking a class to learn how to use and **interpret** sign language.

When might you need someone to interpret for you?

english to spanish

perplexed

The complicated math problem **perplexed** Joshua for many hours.

What problems or puzzles have perplexed you the most?

Build Your Word List Reread the "Setting" on page 133. Circle the word *creating*. In your writer's notebook, use a word web to write more forms of the word. For example, write *creative*. Use an online or print dictionary to find more related words. Then identify their meaning, and use them in sentences.

precise

The nurse made a **precise** measurement of June's height.

What other tasks require someone to be precise?

_____

_____

reconsider

After Cara placed her chess piece, Greta had to **reconsider** her next move.

What is something that might make you reconsider a choice?

_____

_____

suspicious

The dog's owner became **suspicious** when he saw paw prints leading to the chair.

What behavior might make you suspicious of something?

_____

_____

Adages and Proverbs

Adages and proverbs are traditional sayings that are often repeated. You can usually use surrounding words and sentences to help you understand the meaning of an unfamiliar saying.

🔍 FIND TEXT EVIDENCE

On page 133, the narrator of "Where's Brownie?" disagrees with an adage, "Two heads are better than one." In this case, the "two heads" are her own and her twin's. The saying must mean that two people can solve a problem better than one person. However, since her twin "makes problems worse," the narrator probably prefers to figure out things on her own.

Narrator: Whoever claimed that "two heads are better than one" never met my twin sister.

Your Turn Use context clues to explain the meanings of these adages and proverbs from "Where's Brownie?"

"out of sight, out of mind," page 135 _____

_____

"absence makes the heart grow fonder," page 135

_____

Visualize

Each scene in a play includes a setting description. The setting tells where the scene takes place. When you read a play, it is helpful to visualize, or picture, the setting of the scene, the characters, and the characters' actions.

FIND TEXT EVIDENCE

When you read the setting description for Scene One of "Where's Brownie?" on page 133, you may have to slow down and take time to picture what is happening.

> Page 133
>
> Scene One
>
> *Setting: A two-person bedroom in an apartment. SAM sits at a messy desk, creating a poster. EVAN works at a clean desk. Nearby are an empty terrarium and a paper bag that is wet and torn at the bottom.*
>
> **Narrator**: Whoever claimed that "two heads are better than one" never met my twin sister. Half the time, she makes problems worse rather than better. Like when we lost Brownie, our pet chameleon . . .
> (*ALEX enters. SAM and EVAN quickly cover up their work.*)
> **Alex**: How was the science fair? Did everyone like Brownie?

First, I have to picture the room and characters, and I wonder what kind of poster they are making. Also, the sight of an empty terrarium and a wet, torn bag makes me curious as to how all the events are connected.

Your Turn Why is it important that Nicky is playing near the fountain in Scene Two? Visualize the events to help you. As you read, remember to use the strategy Visualize.

Structural Elements

The selection "Where's Brownie?" is a mystery play, or drama. Dramas are made up mostly of dialogue among characters. Dramas have one or more acts. Sometimes acts are separated into scenes. Each scene contains setting details and stage directions.

🔍 FIND TEXT EVIDENCE

I can tell that "Where's Brownie?" is a play. It begins with a cast list telling about the characters' relationships. Its structure includes one act which is divided into two scenes. There is a description of the setting for each scene. There are stage directions. We learn most of the story through dialogue.

Page 134

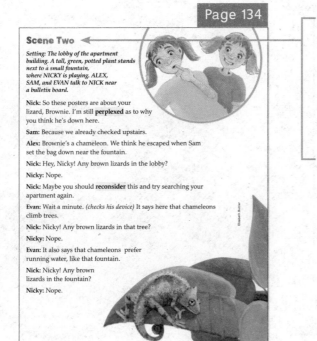

Scene Two

Setting: The lobby of the apartment building. A tall, green, potted plant stands next to a small fountain, where NICKY is playing. ALEX, SAM, and EVAN talk to NICK near a bulletin board.

Nick: So these posters are about your lizard, Brownie. I'm still **perplexed** as to why you think he's down here.

Sam: Because we already checked upstairs.

Alex: Brownie's a chameleon. We think he escaped when Sam set the bag down near the fountain.

Nick: Hey, Nicky! Any brown lizards in the lobby?

Nicky: Nope.

Nick: Maybe you should **reconsider** this and try searching your apartment again.

Evan: Wait a minute. *(checks his device)* It says here that chameleons climb trees.

Nick: Nicky! Any brown lizards in that tree?

Nicky: Nope.

Evan: It also says that chameleons prefer running water, like that fountain.

Nick: Nicky! Any brown lizards in the fountain?

Nicky: Nope.

Scenes

Plays are often divided into scenes that organize the story.

Stage Directions

Stage directions tell actors how to speak dialogue and where they should move.

👥 **COLLABORATE** **Your Turn** How do the events in Scene One of "Where's Brownie?" lead to the events in Scene Two? What do you learn from the stage directions in Scene Two?

_____

_____

_____

Readers to Writers

Writers give specific descriptions of a setting when it is important to the story's plot. For example, the size and the color of the bulletin board is not important to the play's plot, so the board is not described. However, the size and color of the plant is an important element in the plot, so the author gives details about it.

Point of View

In a play, a character who delivers a particular line of dialogue from his or her own point of view is called a **speaker**. In some plays, one speaker may be a **narrator**, who provides information from a point outside of the main action of the play.

🔍 FIND TEXT EVIDENCE

From the first speech of "Where's Brownie?" on page 133, I see a narrator looking back in time to an experience involving her twin sister and a lost pet. This means that she has firsthand knowledge of what happened. I can probably trust what she has to say.

Details	Point of View
Has twin sister who makes "problems worse"	The narrator is one of the sisters. She is caring and reliable, with firsthand knowledge about the event being described.
Had a pet chameleon	
Describes Brownie as "beloved"	

Your Turn Which sister do you think becomes the narrator ten years after the events of the play? Select details that support your answer to place in your graphic organizer on page 141.

Quick Tip

Rereading the narrator's dialogue can help you to understand her feelings and personality. It will also help you understand the conflict between characters. Think about which sister has the most in common with the narrator. This will help you identify the narrator.

Details	Point of View

Respond to Reading

COLLABORATE

Discuss the prompt below. Think about how the writer presents information in the play. Use your notes and graphic organizer.

How does the author help readers solve the mystery along with the characters?

_____

_____

_____

_____

_____

_____

_____

_____

_____

_____

_____

_____

_____

_____

Generate and Clarify Questions

When doing research, a good way to learn information is to **generate questions** about a topic. Sometimes you will need to **clarify questions** in order to find the most useful information. For example, a museum or other institution might have information you need for a research project. First you will ask if they have general information about your topic. If they do, then you might clarify your questions by asking about specific information.

If a museum or institution has information about your topic, what is a clarifying question you could ask?

_____

_____

COLLABORATE

Write a Formal Letter With a partner, research institutions, such as museums, that offer information about the Underground Railroad. Select one and work with your partner to draft a letter requesting more information about the Underground Railroad. For example

- Does the institution have any special exhibits?
- Does the staff have information they can send you, such as pamphlets, booklets, or a brief history?

Discuss the questions you want answered. Make sure they are clear and specific. Then plan your letter. You will be asking for official information, so this is a formal inquiry. After you complete your letter, you will be presenting your work to your class.

A Window into History

*Literature Anthology:
pages 284–293*

? **How does the author show that people have different points of view about turning Grandma J.'s house into a playground?**

COLLABORATE

Talk About It Reread page 287 in the **Literature Anthology**. Turn to your partner and discuss how the author shows the different points of view. Why is Daniel Cruz important to this scene?

Cite Text Evidence What words and phrases tell how each character feels about the house being turned into a playground? Write text evidence in the chart.

Text Evidence	What It Shows

Write The author shows that people have different point of views by _____

_____

_____

Make Inferences

In plays, the characters' names appear before their dialogue. Look for key words and phrases in the dialogue to infer how each character feels about the playground. What do you think the phrases "not right" and "benefit everyone" reveal about the characters' points of view?

How does the author build suspense?

COLLABORATE

Talk About It Reread Act 2, Scene 2 on page 290 in the **Literature Anthology**. Turn to your partner and talk about how the setting details in this scene build suspense.

Cite Text Evidence What details in this scene add to the suspense? Use evidence from the text to support your answers.

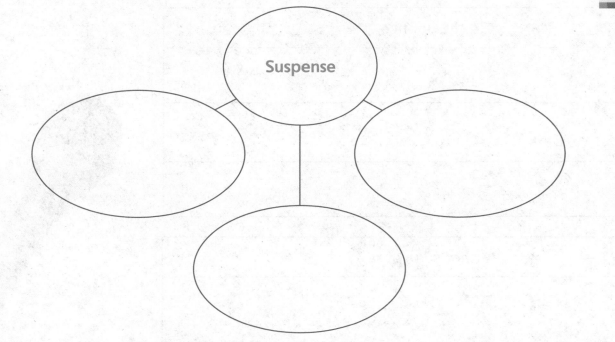

Suspense

Write The author builds suspense in this scene by _____

_____

_____

_____

? **Why does the author have Daniel Cruz interview Dr. Cedric Brown about the history of the house?**

COLLABORATE

Talk About It Reread **Literature Anthology** pages 292 and 293. Turn to your partner and talk about what Dr. Cedric Brown says.

Cite Text Evidence What words and phrases show that Dr. Cedric Brown's interview is important? Write text evidence in the chart.

Quick Tip

To help come up with answers to fill in the chart, think about the decision to not tear down the house. What did Dr. Cedric Brown say that helped with that decision?

Text Evidence

↓

Author's Purpose

Write I know Dr. Cedric Brown's interview is important because _____

_____

_____

_____

C Squared Studios/Getty Images

Respond to Reading

COLLABORATE

Discuss the prompt below. Think about how the writer of a play gives details about the story through dialogue. Use your notes and graphic organizer. Cite, or tell, the act and scene when giving text evidence.

Think about Daniel Cruz's role as a reporter. How does the author use his interviews to help you understand the events in the play?

_____

_____

_____

_____

_____

_____

_____

_____

_____

_____

_____

_____

_____

Quick Tip

Use these sentence starters to help organize your text evidence.

- *The author uses Daniel Cruz to . . .*
- *The interviews help the author to . . .*
- *They help me to understand . . .*

Self-Selected Reading

Choose a text and fill in your writer's notebook with the title, author, and genre. Include a personal response to the text in your writer's notebook.

A Boy, a Horse, and a Fiddle

1   Legend tells of a boy who lived with his grandmother in Mongolia a long time ago and cared for her by herding sheep. A tall, well-built youth with a good and honest heart, he loved to sing and play simple homemade instruments.

2   One day, when the boy was out on the steppes, or the grasslands, tending his sheep, he heard a cry—a soft neigh. By a bush, he found a young colt, as white as snow, without its mother. The boy put a rope around its neck and led it home. In the years that followed, he fed and cared for the animal until it grew into a fine stallion that could run like the wind. The boy also grew and when his work was done, he liked nothing more than to mount his horse and race across the steppes. The horse took much pleasure in listening to the boy sing and play. The two were best friends.

Literature Anthology:
pages 296–299

Reread paragraphs 1 and 2. **Underline** the text evidence that describes the setting. Write your answer here:

1. Mongolia

2. steppes or grasslands

COLLABORATE

Discuss with a partner the key elements of a legend, such as the historical and cultural setting. Talk about what life would be like living in Mongolia long ago. **Circle** the clues that show what life might have been like. How does the setting influence the plot?

The story says

1   The boy was overwhelmed with grief. The following night his horse appeared to him in a dream. Strong and whole, he told the boy:

2   *Make an instrument out of my body. Use my skin to cover the base of the instrument. Use my hair to make two strings, and carve my head out of wood at the top of the fiddle. My ears will guide your sound. I will be with you always as you play and sing, and the music you make will fill people's hearts with joy.*

3   The boy did as he was told. Sure enough, a wonderful, two-stringed instrument was born. It is known as the *morin khurr,* which translates from Mongolian into English as "horse fiddle."

4   Interpret the clues in the image of the morin khurr. The decorations follow the horse's direction to the boy. The strings are made from horse hair. At the top of the fiddle, you will see a pegbox carved in the shape of a horse's head. The tuning pegs on either side are known as the "horse's ears."

COLLABORATE

Reread paragraphs 1 and 2. **Underline** what the horse tells the boy to do with his body. Discuss the text evidence that helps you know that legends such as this one contain fictional elements. Paraphrase the text evidence in your answer.

_____

_____

_____

Reread paragraph 3. **Draw a box** around the words or phrases that tell what instrument was made from the horse's body.

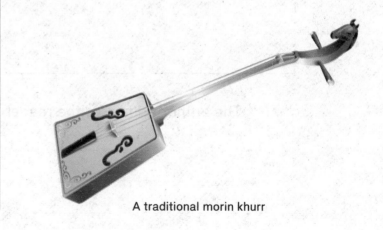

A traditional morin khurr

Why does the author address the reader in the closing paragraph?

Talk About It Reread paragraph 4 on page 149. Analyze the photo of the horse fiddle. With a partner, talk about the ways in which the fiddle matches the description in the story.

Cite Text Evidence What text evidence shows that the morin khurr is based on the legend? Write the text evidence in the chart.

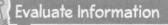
Evaluate Information

A legend is a story passed down through the years. It is often based on real people or real events, but not everything in a legend is true, or possible. Analyze the setting and events that make this story a legend. How does the historical and cultural setting of this story affect the plot?

Detail

Author's Purpose

Write The author addresses the reader in the closing paragraph because

_____

_____

_____

Figurative Language

Figurative language includes similes and metaphors. Authors often use similes and metaphors to help their readers understand and picture ideas, as well as what is being described. A simile uses the words *like* or *as* to compare things. A metaphor makes a comparison without using the words *like* or *as*, for example, *she is a ray of sunshine.*

FIND TEXT EVIDENCE

On page 148 of "A Boy, a Horse, and a Fiddle" the author uses a simile in the second paragraph to help the readers picture the colt that the boy found.

> By a bush, he found a young colt, as white as snow, without its mother.

Your Turn Reread the last sentence of the first paragraph on **Literature Anthology** page 297.

- Is "the chieftain's face turned to stone" a simile or a metaphor? Explain your answer. _____

_____

- Why do you think the author compares the chieftain's face to a stone?

_____

_____

Figurative language is a literary term. In figurative language, words are used in a different way than their usual, or literal, meaning. For example, in the metaphor *The sky is a blanket of stars,* the sky is being compared to a blanket of stars to create an image of a sky full of stars. A literal way to describe the sky could be, *There are many stars in the sky.* Think about how you use figurative and literal language in your own writing.

Text Connections

? How do the poet and authors of *A Window into History: The Mystery of the Cellar Window* and "A Boy, a Horse, and a Fiddle" help you see the benefits of taking a second look?

COLLABORATE

Talk About It Read the poem. Talk with a partner about what the speaker does at the beginning of the poem and what the speaker does at the end.

Cite Text Evidence Work with a partner to **circle** ways the arrow and the song are similar. Then go back and illustrate by **making a mark** in the margin beside the lines that show how the speaker realizes that taking a second look is a good thing to do.

Write **When** they keep looking, the characters in the play and legend and the speaker of the poem discover

_____

_____

_____

_____

_____

_____

Quick Tip

Talk about what the speaker in the poem discovers in the last stanza. How is that different from what happens in the first and second stanzas?

The Arrow and the Song

I shot an arrow into the air,
It fell to earth, I knew not where;
For, so swiftly it flew, the sight
Could not follow it in its flight.

I breathed a song into the air,
It fell to earth, I knew not where;
For who has sight so keen and strong,
That it can follow the flight of song?

Long, long afterward, in an oak
I found the arrow, still unbroke;
And the song, from beginning to end,
I found again in the heart of a friend.

—Henry Wadsworth Longfellow

Present Your Work

COLLABORATE

Discuss how you will present your formal letter requesting information from an institution about the Underground Railroad. Use the Presenting Checklist as you practice your presentation. Discuss the sentence starters below and write your answers.

National Underground Railroad
FREEDOM CENTER

In my research about places that offer information about the Underground Railroad, I learned that _____

_____

_____

I would like to know more about_____

_____

_____

_____

BOB DEMAY/KRT/Newscom

Quick Tip

As you practice your presentation with your partner, think about questions you would ask if you were in the audience. Be prepared to answer these and similar questions.

✓ Presenting Checklist

☐ Plan with your partner how you want to present your letter. Who will read the letter?

☐ Rehearse your presentation.

☐ Speak slowly and clearly during your presentation.

☐ Make eye contact with your audience.

☐ Listen carefully to questions and give answers in full sentences.

Talk About It

Essential Question

How do you express something that is important to you?

COLLABORATE

Look at the photo. How is the man in the photograph expressing what is important to him? How do you express yourself? Talk with a partner about why expressing yourself is important. Write ideas in the web to tell how people express themselves.

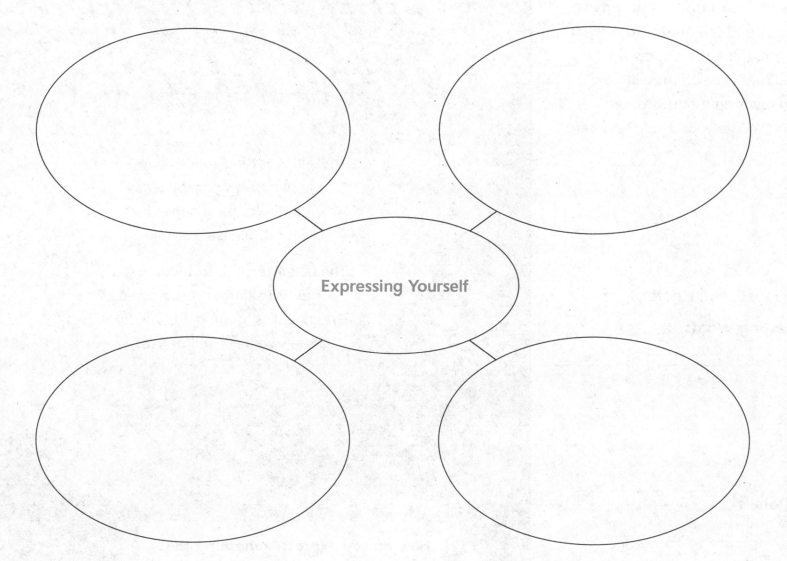

Expressing Yourself

BLAST BACK!
studysync

Go online to **my.mheducation.com** and read the "Expressions of Freedom" Blast. Think about other symbols of hope and freedom. What would you do to express freedom? Then blast back your response.

TAKE NOTES

Before you read the poems, preview the titles and the photos to predict what you think the poems will be about. Your predictions will help you to focus on a purpose for reading. Write your prediction here.

_____

_____

_____

_____

As you read, make note of:

Interesting Words _____

_____

_____

_____

_____

Key Details _____

_____

_____

_____

_____

How Do I Hold the Summer?

The sun is setting sooner now,
   My swimsuit's packed away.
How do I hold the summer fast,
   Or ask it, please, to stay?

The lake like cold, forbidding glass—
   The last sailboat has crossed.
Green leaves, gone gold, fall, float away—
   Here's winter's veil of frost

Essential Question

?

How do you express something that is important to you?

Read three ways that poets express what matters to them.

I thought of ice and barren limbs—
    Last winter's snow so deep!
I know I cannot ball up light,
    And green grass just won't keep,

So I'll search for signs of summer,
    Hold memories of each—
Soft plumes of brown pressed in a book,
    The pit of one ripe peach,

Each instance of a cricket's chirp,
    And every bird's sweet call,
And store them up in a poem to read
    When snow begins to fall.

— Maya Jones

FIND TEXT EVIDENCE

Read

Page 156

Simile and Metaphor

Circle the line that makes a comparison about the lake. What two things are compared?

Page 156

Make Inferences

Why has the last sailboat crossed?

Page 157

Theme

Draw boxes around the sounds heard at the end of the poem. Why does the speaker mention these sounds?

Reread

Author's Craft

Do you think "How Do I Hold the Summer?" is a good title for this poem? Why or why not?

FIND TEXT EVIDENCE 🔍

Read

Page 158

Alliteration

Circle the words that repeat beginning consonant sounds in the same line. What effect does this repetition have on the reader?

_____

_____

_____

Page 158

Theme

What is the poet's message about catching a fly?

_____

_____

_____

Reread

Author's Craft

Why did the poet use short lines to describe the action in the poem?

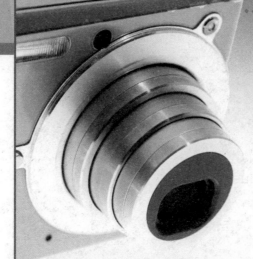

Catching a Fly

It lighted, uninvited
upon the china plate
next to the peas.

No hand I raised
nor finger flicked
but rather found a lens

framed, focused,
zoomed in, held
the hands, still—

the appearance of hands,
like two fine threads, caught
plotting, planning—

greedy goggle eyes, webbed wings
like me, invading—
but no time to pause, he'd go—

and right at the last
instead of a swat,
I snapped!

— Ken Kines

WHEN I DANCE

Always wanna break out,
   use my arms and legs
      to shout!

On any dark day
   that doesn't go
      exactly my way—

I bust a move,
   get a groove,
      feet feel the ground—

That slap's
   the only sound
      slap, pound

my body needs to charge,
   I play my tracks,
      I make it large

to take myself away!
   Nothing else
      I need to say.

— T. C. Arcaro

Make Connections

Compare the forms of expression in the poems to the way you express what is important to you. Talk about whether your prediction on page 156 was confirmed.

POETRY

FIND TEXT EVIDENCE 🔍

Read

Page 159

Stanza and Meter

Draw a box around two sections that best express why dancing is important to the speaker. Explain your choice.

_____

_____

_____

_____

_____

Reread

Author's Craft

How does the poet help you visualize what is expressed in the poem?

Fluency

Take turns reading the first stanza of "When I Dance." Discuss how fast the poet wants you to read.

Vocabulary

Use the example sentences to talk with a partner about each word. Then answer the questions.

barren

The **barren** land did not have a single tree or bush.

What is another word or phrase for barren?

Another word for barren is dead or death.

expression

James wrote songs as an **expression** of his thoughts about friendship.

Name another form of artistic expression.

You can snow or tell who you are.

meaningful

The students had a **meaningful** discussion about how to protect the environment.

What meaningful discussions have you had?

I have had a meaningful discussion about my grades.

plumes

Each year, peacocks shed their beautiful tail **plumes** and grow new ones.

What beautiful plumes have you seen?

A beautifull plume that I snow was a bird.

Poetry Terms

lyric

Some poets write **lyric** poetry that describes their feelings about nature and seasons.

Would you prefer to read a lyric poem about spring or fall?

I would perker to read a lyric about full.

alliteration

"Lou's lamb" shows **alliteration** because the same consonant sound begins two or more words.

Give another example of alliteration, using any consonant.

Sally Sold Seeshells by the Seelshore.

meter

Rita tapped her fingers in rhythm to the **meter** of the poem as she read it aloud.

Say the first line of *Jack and Jill* to yourself. What is the meter?

There ure 4 meters in Jacu and Jin went up the mil.

stanza

In some poems, each **stanza** may have four lines.

How is a stanza like a paragraph?

Astunza B like a nara grugh because it is a group of lines.

 Build Your Word List Pick a word from any of the poems that you had a hard time pronouncing. A print or online dictionary can show you how to say the word. Write the word and its pronunciation and definition in your writer's notebook.

Simile and Metaphor

A **simile** makes a comparison using the words *like* or *as*: legs like sticks. A **metaphor** makes a comparison without using the words *like* or *as*: stick legs. These comparisons are figurative language because they are not used in a literal sense. Writers use them to create a vivid effect.

FIND TEXT EVIDENCE

The fifth stanza of "Catching a Fly" has the metaphor "greedy goggle eyes" that compares the fly's eyes to goggles, focused on food.

> greedy goggle eyes, webbed wings
> like me, invading—
> but no time to pause, he'd go—

Your Turn Reread the fourth stanza of "Catching a Fly." What comparison does the simile make?

the appearance of hands,
like two fine threads, caught
plotting, planning—

_____

_____

Stanza and Meter

A **stanza** is a section of the poem that expresses a key idea. Together these ideas help form a poem's main message. Poets may also use sound devices, such as **meter**, also called rhythm. In poetry, meter is a regular pattern of sounds in a line.

FIND TEXT EVIDENCE

Reread the poem "How Do I Hold the Summer?" on pages 156 and 157. Identify the stanzas in the poem and think about how they are alike.

Page 157

So I'll search for signs of summer,
    Hold memories of each—
Soft plumes of brown pressed in a book,
    The pit of one ripe peach,

Each instance of a cricket's chirp,
    And every bird's sweet call,
And store them up in a poem to read
    When snow begins to fall.

Each stanza has four lines and contains a key idea.

An equal number of beats in the lines creates a regular meter, or rhythm.

Your Turn Identify the key idea of each stanza of "How Do I Hold the Summer?" How do these ideas help form the poem's main message?

_____

_____

_____

> **Quick Tip**
>
> A poem's title can give you many ideas about the poem. Think about the title of this poem. What images does it create? Does it tell you who or what the subject of the poem is? Does it give clues to the poem's main message?

Lyric and Free Verse

Lyric poetry expresses personal thoughts and feelings. It often has a regular meter, or pattern of sounds. Lyric poetry may be arranged in stanzas and may contain rhyme and alliteration.

Free verse expresses ideas and feelings with carefully chosen words. It has no set rhyming pattern, meter, or line length. Free verse may include alliteration and stanzas.

FIND TEXT EVIDENCE

I can tell that "How Do I Hold the Summer?" is a lyric poem because it expresses the speaker's thoughts and feelings. It also includes rhyme, a regular meter, stanzas, and alliteration.

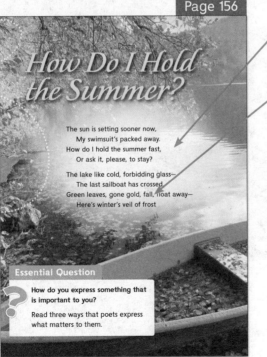

Page 156

How Do I Hold the Summer?

The sun is setting sooner now,
My swimsuit's packed away.
How do I hold the summer fast,
Or ask it, please, to stay?

The lake like cold, forbidding glass—
The last sailboat has crossed.
Green leaves, gone gold, fall, float away—
Here's winter's veil of frost

Essential Question

How do you express something that is important to you?

Read three ways that poets express what matters to them.

The poem expresses feelings and includes rhyme.

The poem contains alliteration, with words that begin with the consonants g *and* f.

Your Turn Reread the poem "Catching a Fly" on page 158. Decide if it is an example of lyric or free verse poetry. What elements do you see?

_____

_____

_____

_____

Theme

The **theme** of a poem is the message, or big idea, that the poet wishes to tell the reader. Identifying poetic elements and key details can help you determine a poem's theme. Sometimes, a poem can have multiple themes.

FIND TEXT EVIDENCE

All three poems have speakers who express something important to them, but each poem has a different theme. I'll reread "How Do I Hold the Summer?" and look for key details to determine a theme.

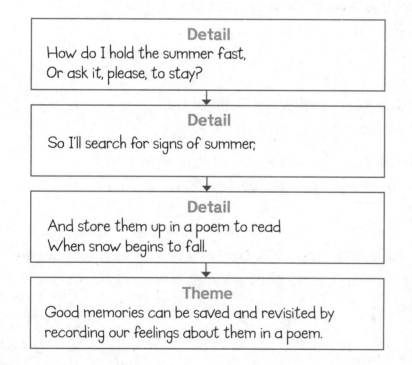

> **Detail**
> How do I hold the summer fast,
> Or ask it, please, to stay?
>
> ↓
>
> **Detail**
> So I'll search for signs of summer,
>
> ↓
>
> **Detail**
> And store them up in a poem to read
> When snow begins to fall.
>
> ↓
>
> **Theme**
> Good memories can be saved and revisited by recording our feelings about them in a poem.

Your Turn Reread the poem "When I Dance." List key details in the graphic organizer on page 165. Use the details to figure out one theme of the poem.

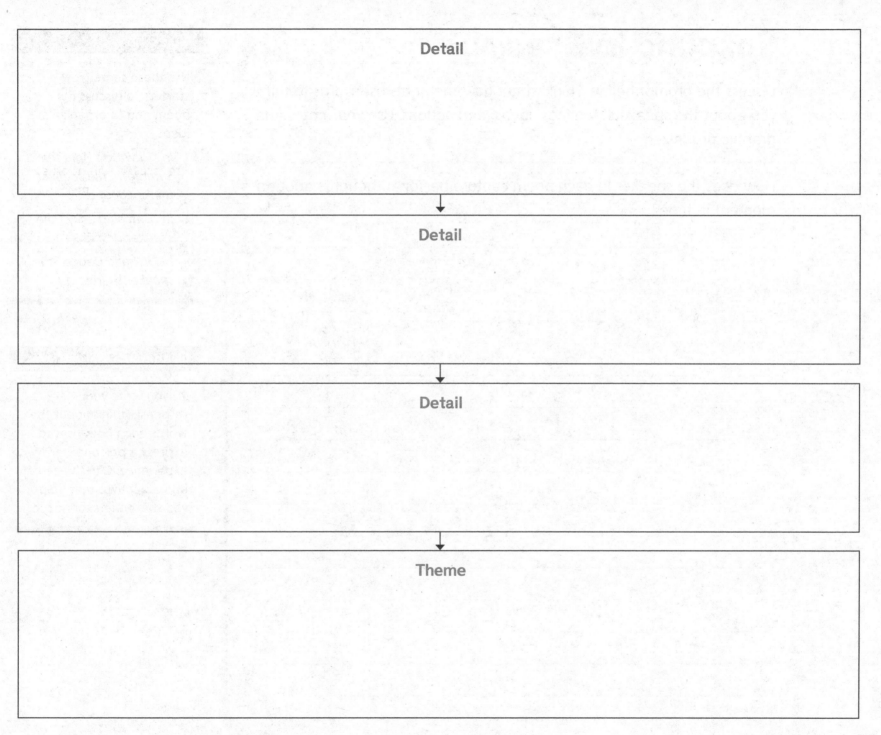

Detail

Detail

Detail

Theme

Respond to Reading

Discuss the prompt below. Think about how the poets use words to tell you about the speakers' feelings, ideas, and actions. Use your notes and graphic organizer.

How does the speaker in each poem capture personal thoughts about a moment in time?

_____
_____
_____
_____
_____
_____
_____
_____
_____
_____
_____
_____
_____
_____
_____
_____

Quick Tip

Use these sentence starters to discuss the poem and to organize ideas.

- In "How Do I Hold the Summer?" the speaker thinks about . . .
- In "Catching a Fly," the speaker describes . . .
- In "When I Dance," the speaker shares . . .

Grammar Connections

As you write your response, think about the words each poet uses to express a personal experience. Cite the verbs and adjectives that help you share the experience.

Relevant Information

Before you research a topic, you need to choose your focus. Then you can more easily gather **relevant information**. *Relevant* means that the information is connected to your topic. Some information you find may be interesting, but it may not fit with your focus. Do the following as you start to identify relevant information:

- With a trusted adult, preview a website, book, or article before reading to see if it has the information you need.
- Skim the content, quickly examining the text. Then read more carefully if you see information you will likely use for your project.

As you quickly read through sources, what would you look for in deciding if the information is relevant to your topic?

_____

_____

Create a Timeline With a group, research the origins and significance of major national holidays in the United States. Look for the following:

- On what date did the holiday first become a national holiday?
- Who was the president who signed the bill that made it official?
- Why was it made a national holiday?

With your group, decide how you will research each holiday. Then plan what to include on your timeline and how you will create it. After you complete your timeline, you will be presenting your work to your class.

Tech Tip

There are many websites that do not provide reliable information. Sometimes, the facts have not been checked. Usually, websites that end in *.gov* or *.edu* are good sites to gather information from.

National Holidays

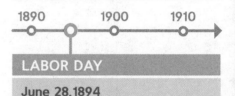

1890   1900   1910

LABOR DAY

June 28, 1894
Congress passed a bill; President Cleveland signed it into law

The image above shows a part of a timeline about national holidays.

Words Free as Confetti

? **How does the poet's use of free verse create the poem's mood?**

Literature Anthology:
pages 300–302

Talk About It Reread **Literature Anthology** page 300 out loud with a partner. Talk about how the poem makes you feel.

Cite Text Evidence What words and phrases does the poet use to create mood? Write text evidence in the chart below.

Make Inferences

A poet carefully chooses what words or phrases to include in a poem. What inference can you make about why the poet includes Spanish words in the poem?

Text Evidence	How It Creates Mood

Write The poet uses free verse to create the poem's mood by _____

_____

_____

_____

Dreams

? In "Dreams," how does the poet use repetition and meter to help you understand his message?

COLLABORATE

Talk About It Reread **Literature Anthology** page 302. Turn to your partner and discuss what you notice about the way the poem is organized and how that relates to the theme.

Cite Text Evidence What phrases are repeated and how do they help the poet share his message? Write text evidence in the chart.

Text Evidence	Organization	Effect on Reader

Write The poet uses repetition and meter to _____

_____

_____

_____

Quick Tip

Look for phrases that are used more than once in the poem. These phrases may express the poet's message. Meter, also called rhythm, and repetition can work together to help you better understand the poem's theme.

Synthesize Information

What are the two things that Langston Hughes compares to dreams that die or are let go? What images and feelings do these things bring to mind? How do they help you understand the theme of the poem?

Respond to Reading

COLLABORATE

Discuss the prompt below. Reread both poems, read them out loud, and notice key words or phrases to inform your answer. Use your notes and graphic organizer.

How do the poets use repetition and meter to help convey the theme of their poems?

_____

_____

_____

_____

_____

_____

_____

_____

_____

_____

_____

_____

Quick Tip

Use these sentence starters to organize your text evidence.

- *In her poem, Pat Mora . . .*
- *Langston Hughes uses repetition to . . .*
- *This helps me understand the poets' messages because . . .*

Self-Selected Reading

Choose a text and fill in your writer's notebook with the title, author, and genre. Include a personal response to the text in your writer's notebook. When you make a personal connection, you might think of an experience you had that is similar to what you read.

A Story of How a Wall Stands

? **How does the poet use dialogue to help you understand how the speaker's father feels about his work?**

Literature Anthology: pages 304–305

Talk About It Reread **Literature Anthology** pages 304–305. Talk with a partner about how the speaker's father describes how he built a wall.

Cite Text Evidence What words and phrases help you figure out how the father feels about his work? Write evidence in the chart.

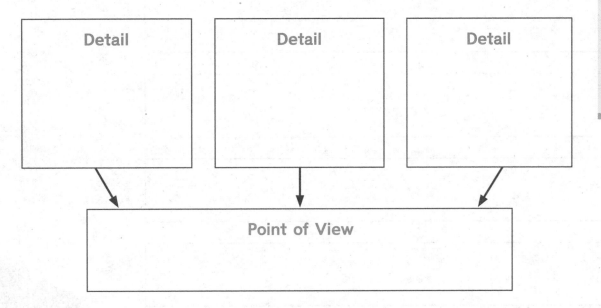

| Detail | Detail | Detail |

Point of View

Evaluate Information

Reread just the father's dialogue. Think about his words. How does his description of how he works add meaning to how a wall is built? What does this reveal about the speaker's father?

Write The poet uses dialogue to show that the speaker's father feels _____

_____

_____

_____

? **How does the poet help you see the speaker's point of view about his father?**

COLLABORATE

Talk About It Reread the poem on **Literature Anthology** pages 304 and 305. With a partner, discuss how the speaker feels about his father's work.

Cite Text Evidence What words in the dialogue show how the speaker feels about his father's work? Write text evidence in the chart.

Quick Tip

Reread the last stanza on page 305. Notice how the poet repeats the father's dialogue using the words "a long, long time." What does this tell you about the speaker's point of view?

Building a Wall

↓

↓

↓

Write The poet uses dialogue to help me understand the speaker's point of view by _____

_____

_____

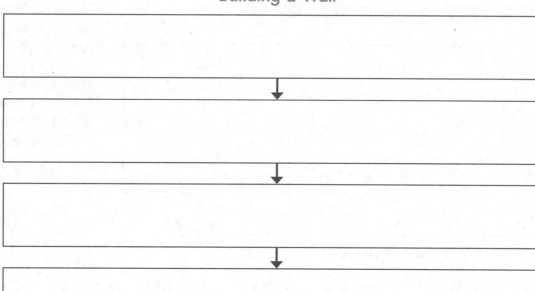

Voice

A poet creates a speaker to tell a poem and gives the speaker a voice. **Voice** is the speaker's specific personality. Part of voice is tone, or the attitude toward a topic. The poet's word choices, such as repetition, contribute to the speaker's voice.

FIND TEXT EVIDENCE

In "A Story of How a Wall Stands" on pages 304 and 305 in the **Literature Anthology,** the speaker's father builds a stone wall as he explains to the speaker how he makes it strong. *Stone* is used many times in both the speaker's and the father's words. This repetition adds an attitude of strength and patience to the speaker's voice.

Your Turn Reread the last stanza of the poem on page 305.

• What words are repeated in this stanza and from earlier in the poem?

_____

_____

• What attitude or tone do you hear in the speaker's voice? How does the repetition of words contribute to this voice? _____

_____

_____

_____

_____

_____

Readers to Writers

There are many ways to add voice to your writing, including repetition. Think about your feelings and attitude toward your topic. Choose words that express what you feel.

Text Connections

? **How do the sculptors of this statue and the poets of "Words Free as Confetti" and "A Story of How a Wall Stands" express their ideas?**

Talk About It Look at the photograph. Read the caption. With a partner, talk about how the sculptors expressed their ideas through art.

Cite Text Evidence **Draw boxes** around details in the photograph that tell you something about Abraham Lincoln. **Circle** clues that show the message the sculptors wanted to express.

Write The sculptors and poets express

their ideas by _____

_____

_____

_____

_____

_____

_____

_____

_____

Carol M. Highsmith's America, Library of Congress, Prints and Photographs Division.

This bronze statue depicts Abraham Lincoln and his horse, Old Bob, at the Lincoln Summer Home in Washington, D.C. It was created in 2009 by Ivan Schwartz, Stuart Williamson, and Jiwoong Cheh.

Expression and Rate

Quick Tip

When deciding on a rate for reading a poem, preview the whole poem. The speaker may change from excitement to a quieter feeling. So, you may want to read faster and then slow down to show the change.

A poem reveals a poet's feelings and thoughts about an idea, experience, or a moment in time. Reading a poem aloud with **expression** gives life to those feelings and thoughts. The **rate** or speed at which you read the poem will also help to express a poem's meaning. A poem that expresses excitement or happiness might be read quickly. If the poem seems sad or thoughtful, you might read more slowly.

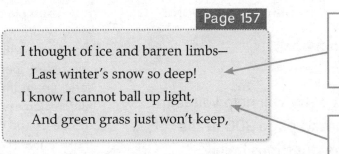

Page 157

I thought of ice and barren limbs—
   Last winter's snow so deep!
I know I cannot ball up light,
   And green grass just won't keep,

The exclamation point is a clue to emphasize "so deep" to show feelings about a memory.

Read the last two lines at a slightly faster rate to show frustration.

Your Turn Turn back to page 159. Take turns reading aloud the poem "When I Dance" with a partner. Think about how you felt when you first read the poem. Express these feelings and energy in your expression and reading rate.

Afterward, think about how you did. Complete these sentences.

I remembered to _____

_____

Next time, I will _____

_____

Literature Anthology pages 300–301

Expert Model

Features of a Free Verse Poem

A free verse poem expresses the thoughts and feelings of the speaker, the narrator of the poem. A free verse poem differs from other types of poetry. A free verse poem

- has no set line lengths and usually does not rhyme

- often includes imagery created by the poet's carefully chosen words

- may include sound devices and figurative language

Analyze an Expert Model Studying free verse poetry will help you learn how to write a free verse poem of your own. **Reread** page 300 in the **Literature Anthology.** Write your answers to the questions below.

How do you know that "Words Free as Confetti" is a free verse poem?

_____

_____

_____

What else do you notice about "Words Free as Confetti" that makes it different from other poems you have read? _____

_____

_____

Word Wise

In the fourth line of the poem, the author uses the words "plump plums." This is an example of alliteration, with words that begin with the same consonant sound. Free verse poems may include alliteration as a sound device. Sound devices make a poem more musical sounding when read aloud.

Plan: Choose Your Topic

Brainstorm With a partner, discuss things that make you happy. These could be things you enjoy doing, people you like, or places you like to go. Use these sentence starters to get started.

Something that makes me happy is . . .

It makes me happy because . . .

Writing Prompt Choose one idea from your discussion and use it as the topic for a free verse poem.

I will write my free verse poem about _____

Purpose and Audience A free verse poem expresses feelings and thoughts. Circle your purpose for writing a free verse poem.

  to inform, or teach   to entertain   to persuade, or convince

Think about your audience. Who will read or listen to your poem?

My audience will be _____ .

I will use _____ language.

Plan In your writer's notebook, make a web to plan your poem. Fill in the idea and at least one detail.

Quick Tip

As the poet, you need to decide who the speaker of your poem is. A poem's speaker is like a story's narrator. For example, you are in the fifth grade, but you can write your poem as if a younger person is speaking it.

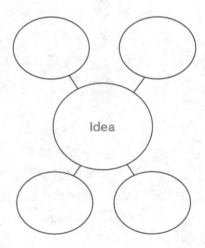

Idea

Plan: Imagery

Brainstorm Descriptive Details Once you have decided on your topic and thought of some details you plan to include, you need to think carefully about how to describe them. One of the goals of free verse poetry is to create an image in the reader's mind. The language you use will help you do this. As you write your first draft, ask yourself these questions:

• Am I telling my readers something or am I showing them?

• How can I use words effectively to create a picture in the reader's mind?

• What descriptive language would make this part more interesting?

Think of two descriptive details you could use in your free verse poem.

1 _____

_____

2 _____

_____

 Take Notes Once you've decided on the details you will include in your poem, fill in the rest of your web. If you need more space to write your details, use a separate sheet of paper in your writer's notebook to continue your notes.

Draft

Visual Arrangement One feature of free verse poetry is that it can be arranged on the page in creative ways. Thinking carefully about your line breaks is one way to consider the visual arrangement of your poem, or the way the words are organized on the page. Read the example below from "Grandpa's Shed" and pay close attention to the visual arrangement.

> Grandpa merely dips his brush,
> Paints a horse and hound.
> "The horse I harnessed as a boy,
> Dog was mine too."

Now use the above excerpt as a model to write some lines that could go in your own free verse poem. Think carefully about your line breaks and how you organize the words on the page.

_____

_____

_____

_____

_____

Write a Draft Use your web to help you write your draft in your writer's notebook. Remember to use plenty of imagery.

Grammar Connection

As you write your draft, use correct subject-verb agreement with indefinite pronouns. Look at the phrase that follows the pronoun to decide whether to use a singular or plural verb: *All of the sky is blue. All of the clouds are white.*

Revise

Figurative Language Poets often use figurative language to make their poems more creative. Figurative language includes similes, metaphors, and personification. Read the poem below. Then revise it to improve word choice by using figurative language and combining ideas for clarity.

> When I skate
>
> on the level, flat ice
>
> I go so fast.
>
> On the ice,
>
> I jump and spin.

Revision Revise your draft, and check that you use some figurative language. Improve word choice by combining ideas for clarity.

Peer Conferences

COLLABORATE

Review a Draft Listen carefully as a partner reads his or her work aloud. Take notes about what you liked and what was difficult to follow. Begin by telling what you liked about the draft. Ask questions that will help the writer think more about the writing. Make suggestions that you think will make the writing stronger. Use these sentence starters.

I enjoyed this part of your draft because . . .

You might add some figurative language to . . .

I have a question about . . .

This part is unclear to me. Can you explain why . . . ?

Partner Feedback After your partner gives you feedback on your draft, write one of the suggestions that you will use in your revision. Refer to the rubric on page 183 as you give feedback.

Based on my partner's feedback, I will _____

_____

_____

After you finish giving each other feedback, reflect on the peer conference. What was helpful? What might you do differently next time?

Revision As you revise your draft, use the Revising Checklist to help you figure out what text you may need to move, elaborate on, or delete. Remember to use the rubric on page 183 to help you with your revision.

✔ Revising Checklist

- [ ] Does my writing fit my purpose and audience?
- [ ] What details can I add or delete to make my poem clearer?
- [ ] Do I have enough imagery?
- [ ] Have I used figurative language?

Edit and Proofread

When you **edit** and **proofread** your writing, you look for and correct mistakes in spelling, punctuation, capitalization, and grammar. Reading through a revised draft multiple times can help you make sure you're catching any errors. Use the checklist below to edit your poem.

✔ Editing Checklist

☐ Are all homophones used and spelled correctly?

☐ Are all my pronouns correct?

☐ Are proper nouns capitalized?

☐ Are quotation marks used correctly?

☐ Are all words spelled correctly?

Grammar Connections

Even though free verse poetry has very few rules, it still may need punctuation. When you proofread your poem, make sure that the poem is free of errors in punctuation.

List two mistakes you found as you proofread your poem.

1 _____

_____

2 _____

_____

Publish, Present, and Evaluate

Publishing When you **publish** your writing, you create a clean, neat final copy that is free of mistakes. As you write your final draft be sure to write legibly in cursive. Check that you are holding your pencil or pen correctly.

Presentation When you are ready to **present** your work, rehearse your presentation. Use the Presenting Checklist to help you.

Evaluate After you publish your writing, use the rubric below to **evaluate** your writing.

What did you do successfully? _____

What needs more work? _____

_____

✔ Presenting Checklist

☐ Stand up straight.

☐ Look at the audience.

☐ Speak clearly and loudly enough so that everyone can hear you.

☐ Speak with expression and use natural gestures.

4	3	2	1
• the free verse poem is clearly about something the writer enjoys • successfully uses imagery to create a picture in the reader's mind • effectively uses figurative language	• the free verse poem is about something the writer enjoys • uses some imagery that creates a picture in the reader's mind • some figurative language is used	• the free verse poem is unclear about something the writer enjoys • uses very little imagery • very little figurative language is used	• the free verse poem is not about something the writer enjoys • does not use imagery • no figurative language is used

Digital Tools

For more information about presenting, watch the "How to Give a Presentation" video. Go to **my.mheducation.com**.

Spiral Review

You have learned new skills and strategies in Unit 4 that will help you read more critically. Now it is time to practice what you have learned.

- Photographs and Captions
- Author's Point of View
- Structural Elements: Drama
- Make Inferences
- Adages and Proverbs

Connect to Content
- Analyze Flashback
- "Droughtbusters"

Read the selection and choose the best answer to each question.

CESAR CHAVEZ:
Hero of the Working People

1 There are people who devote their lives to helping others and making the world a better place. Cesar Chavez was one of those people. Cesar Estrada Chavez was born in Yuma, Arizona, on March 31, 1927. He grew up on a small farm owned by his grandparents. The children helped with the farm, but they had time to play and explore the Arizona landscape, as well.

2 Then, in 1938, life changed for the Chavez family. A drought hit Yuma, and the Chavez farm could not raise enough crops or livestock. They could not pay the taxes on their farm, and they lost it. The family was forced to leave their home. They headed for California where they became migrant workers. Migrant workers are people who work on a farm or ranch for short periods, usually during harvest time.

3 After Cesar finished 8th grade, he had to stop going to school to help his family full time in the fields. He became aware of the harsh conditions that migrant workers endured. He spent long hours bent over in the hot sun and received low pay. Migrant workers lived in camps that had unclean water and were infested with insects. Workers were also exposed to pesticides and other harmful chemicals.

4   Chavez joined the U.S. Navy in 1944. After two years in the Navy, Chavez returned to California and the difficult life of a migrant worker. He became involved with people trying to improve conditions for migrant workers. In 1962, along with a woman named Dolores Huerta, he founded a labor union called the National Farm Workers Association.

5   Chavez led protests and strikes to call attention to the migrant workers' problems. A strike is when workers refuse to work. In the mid-1960s, Chavez's union joined Filipinos who harvested grapes in a strike for better wages. During the strike, Chavez got people all across America to boycott, or stop buying, California grapes. Because of this boycott, wages and other conditions improved for the workers.

6   In 1971, the National Farm Workers Association became the United Farm Workers (UFW). Chavez led boycotts against lettuce growers and other farm businesses. The union was able to negotiate higher pay and benefits for farm workers. In addition, growers were no longer allowed to use dangerous pesticides that could harm workers.

7   After thirty years of fighting for the rights of farm workers, Chavez died on April 23, 1993. He left behind improved working conditions for migrant workers in California, Texas, Arizona, and Florida. His work to protect migrant workers still continues today. He is remembered by many as a hero of the working people.

In 1985, Chavez again asked people to boycott grapes to get growers to set safe standards for pesticide use. A pesticide is a substance used to kill insects. ▲

SHOW WHAT YOU LEARNED

1. The author's point of view that Cesar Chavez is a hero is best supported by —
   - A the hard work performed by migrant laborers
   - B the description of improved conditions for migrant workers
   - C information about Chavez living on a farm as a child
   - D information about Chavez leaving school after 8th grade

Quick Tip

Start by crossing out the answer choices you know are not correct. Then reread the text to decide which of the remaining chocies is correct.

2. Based on the selection, what can readers infer about Chavez?
   - F Chavez cared greatly about justice.
   - G Chavez enjoyed being in the Navy.
   - H Chavez became ill from pesticides.
   - J Chavez became an elected politician who helped farm workers.

3. The photograph of the 1965 march conveys the message that —
   - A Chavez's cause was not supported
   - B people had trouble sharing their message
   - C supporters were mostly older men
   - D the protest drew a crowd of people

4. What does the caption of the 1985 photograph indicate?
   - F There are many plans Chavez used to make social change.
   - G Many people did not support boycotts so Chavez gave them up.
   - H The boycott plan was a favorite of Chavez's over the years.
   - J The author disapproves of Chavez's plans for social change.

Read the selection and choose the best answer to each question.

A DRAMATIC DISCOVERY

ACT 1, SCENE 1

SETTING: Grandma's living room.
Grandma is sitting in a chair working on her laptop computer. Vincent and Maria come into the room.

MARIA: Hi, Grandma. We need your help. (*smiles*) As usual.

GRANDMA: (*looking concerned*) Is everything okay? What's wrong?

MARIA: (*smiling*) Don't worry. Nothing's wrong! We just need to find costumes for the community theater play. We both got parts! The play takes place forty years ago . . .

VINCENT: (*interrupting Maria*) Yeah, and Mom said she thought you might have some old clothes you could donate for the play. She says you never throw anything away.

GRANDMA: (*frowning*) Hmm. I do throw away *useless* things. But, go check in the attic. There should be a couple of boxes there and some chairs you can use. And congratulations on getting parts! It was brave of you to try out! As I always say, "Fortune favors the bold!"

ACT 1, SCENE 2

SETTING: The attic. There is old furniture such as chairs, lamps, and small tables. There is also a pile of blankets next to a few stacks of boxes.
Maria and Vincent walk into the attic. Vincent goes to look at the chairs. Maria heads towards the boxes near the blankets.

MARIA: I'll look. (*bangs her leg on something*) Ouch! What's this? (*She moves blankets to reveal a trunk, and then opens the trunk and pulls out an old hat and dress.*) Hey, this is perfect. (*She looks in the trunk again and pulls out a smaller box. She opens the box and pulls out a small poster.*) Vincent come here! You'll want to see this.

(Vincent goes to look at the poster.)

VINCENT: (*surprised*) That's Grandma! She starred in the community play when she was our age! Wow! I didn't know she acted.

MARIA: Me, neither. I wonder if we can convince her to join the play now?

VINCENT: We can try, but I bet she'll say she's too busy. She's always busy.

ACT 2

SETTING: A little while later in Grandma's kitchen. *Grandma is busy making bread. Maria and Vincent come into the room. Vincent is holding the poster.*

GRANDMA *(without looking up)* Did you find anything useful?

VINCENT: Yep. We found a hat, a dress, and this. *(Grandma looks up and sees the poster.)*

GRANDMA: Oh my, that was a long time ago!

VINCENT: I bet you were good. I bet you would still be good! Not all the parts in the play are cast. Will you please try out?

GRANDMA: Oh, I don't think so. I have a lot to do. I am very busy.

MARIA: Please . . . It would be so much more fun if you were there. Join us!

GRANDMA: Besides, I haven't acted in years. I doubt I would be very good anymore.

VINCENT: You're always saying "<u>Fortune favors the bold</u>." Be bold! Try out. We think you will be great.

GRANDMA: *(takes a long look at her grandchildren, and then slowly smiles)* Well. Okay. Bold it is!

VINCENT and MARIA: *(grinning)* Hurray!

1 Act 1 of the play has two scenes because —

A Grandma goes to the kitchen

B the setting changes ✓

C there are two characters in the second scene

D there are a lot of stage directions

2 In Act 1, Scene 1, what can be inferred about Maria's opinion?

F Her grandmother never throws anything out.

G Her grandmother worries too much.

X J

H It will be fun to have her grandmother in the play.

J Her grandmother can be helpful.

3 What does the proverb <u>Fortune favors the bold</u> mean?

A It is better to be cautious and take things slowly in order to succeed at something.

B It is good luck to be in a play.   ✓

C If you are brave and try things, you will often find success.

D Family members should do favors for each other so they will have good fortune.

4 From Maria and Vincent's dialogue you can tell —

F they often disagree about things

G they are good actors

H they often visit their grandmother   ✓

J they enjoy their grandmother's company

EXTEND YOUR LEARNING

IDENTIFY AND USE PREFIXES AND SUFFIXES

- Many English words contain word parts from Greek and Latin.

- **Prefixes** are added to the beginning of words. **Suffixes** are added to the end of words. Prefixes and suffixes affect words' meanings. Together, the two groups are called **affixes.**

- By learning the meaning of common Greek and Latin affixes, you can figure out the meaning of unfamiliar words and correctly use them in sentences.

- Complete the chart by adding more examples. Choose three words from "More Examples." In your writer's notebook, write each word and its meaning. Use a print or digital dictionary to check your answers. Then use each word in a sentence.

Affix	Meaning	Origin	Example	More Examples
trans-	"across"	Latin	transport	
super-	"above or beyond"	Latin	supermarket	
-ive	"given to" "relating to"	Latin	active	
-logy	"study of"	Greek	biology	

RESEARCH ADAGES AND PROVERBS

Benjamin Franklin (1706–1790) was a Founding Father of the United States. He was also an author, a printer, and an inventor. Franklin published *Poor Richard's Almanack*. An almanac contains facts on many different subjects. Franklin's almanac included adages and proverbs, traditional sayings, that often shared wisdom in a witty way. "Early to bed, early to rise, makes a man healthy, wealthy, and wise." What do you think this saying means?

_____

_____

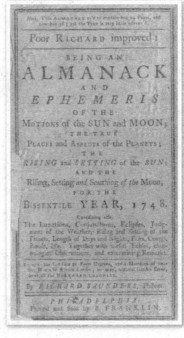

Create your own illustrated book using adages and proverbs. Identify and include an adage or proverb from *Poor Richard's Almanack*. Also include three adages or proverbs of your own. Explain the meanings.

PUNS

Puns are words or phrases used in a witty way that suggest a different meaning. Authors use puns in such a way that two or more meanings apply. For example, "A bicycle can't stand on its own because it is two-tired." The word "tired" is being used to mean both "not having energy" and the tires of the bike.

- Underline the sentence that is a pun. Then explain its meaning.
  "A hard-boiled egg in the morning is hard to beat."
  "A hard-boiled egg in the morning is good to eat."

_____

_____

- In your writer's notebook, use and explain one original pun.

ANALYZE FLASHBACK

A **flashback** occurs when an author interrupts the sequence of story events to return to an earlier event.

- In the **Literature Anthology,** on page 268 of the biography *Rosa,* review the flashback to the 1954 *Brown versus Board of Education* Decision by the United States Supreme Court.

- Research this court case and take notes about the important details.

_____

_____

_____

_____

_____

_____

_____

- With a partner or small group, discuss the author's purpose in using this flashback.

_____

_____

_____

DROUGHTBUSTERS

COLLABORATE

Digital texts often have interactive elements that allow you to click on parts of the text to get more detailed information. They also may have links to videos, articles, and other sites. Log on to **my.mheducation.com** and reread the *Time for Kids* online article "Droughtbusters," including the information found in the interactive elements. Answer the questions below.

Droughtbusters
The world is getting thirstier. How do we keep from going dry?

Time for Kids: "Droughtbusters"

- Why is there a shortage of fresh water around the world? List two causes.

  _____

  _____

- What is Perth in western Australia doing to improve freshwater supplies?

  _____

- What do you predict will be the effect of this technology on future water supplies? Explain your answer.

  _____

  _____

- What is Bangalore, India doing to improve freshwater supplies?

  _____

- Name some other methods, or ways, that places mentioned in the article are increasing freshwater supplies.

  _____

  _____

TRACK YOUR PROGRESS

WHAT DID YOU LEARN?

Use the rubric to evaluate yourself on the skills you learned in this unit.
Write your scores in the boxes below.

4	3	2	1
I can successfully identify all examples of this skill.	I can identify most examples of this skill.	I can identify a few examples of this skill.	I need to work on this skill more.

☐ Point of View

☐ Author's Point of View

☐ Adages and Proverbs

☐ Theme

☐ Prefixes and Suffixes

☐ Simile and Metaphor

Something that I need to work more on is _____ because
_____

_____

_____

Text to Self Think back over the texts that you have read in this unit.
Choose one text and write a short paragraph explaining a personal
connection that you have made to the text.

I made a personal connection to _____ because _____
_____

_____

_____

Present Your Work

COLLABORATE

Discuss how you will present your timeline about the origins of American national holidays. Use the Presenting Checklist as you practice your presentation. Discuss the sentence starters below and write your answers.

Presenting Checklist

- ☐ Plan with your group how you will present your timeline.
- ☐ Rehearse your presentation.
- ☐ Speak slowly and clearly during your presentation.
- ☐ Make eye contact with your audience.
- ☐ Be prepared to answer questions.

In my research about the history of American national holidays, I discovered that _____

_____

_____

I would like to know more about _____

_____

_____